May God
Berth

Sentimental Journey

Poetry and Prose

Bertha Phebus

WESTBOW·
PRESS
A DIVISION OF THOMAS NELSON
& ZONDERVAN

WestBow Press books may be ordered through booksellers or by contacting:

WestBow Press
A Division of Thomas Nelson & Zondervan
1663 Liberty Drive
Bloomington, IN 47403
www.westbowpress.com
1 (866) 928-1240

Because of the dynamic nature of the Internet, any web addresses or links contained in this book may have changed since publication and may no longer be valid. The views expressed in this work are solely those of the author and do not necessarily reflect the views of the publisher, and the publisher hereby disclaims any responsibility for them.

Any people depicted in stock imagery provided by Thinkstock are models, and such images are being used for illustrative purposes only. Certain stock imagery © Thinkstock.

ISBN: 978-1-4908-5121-1 (sc)
ISBN: 978-1-4908-5122-8 (e)

Library of Congress Control Number: 2014916084

Printed in the United States of America.

WestBow Press rev. date: 10/23/2014

Dedication

To God
who has blessed my life
with loved ones
and
precious friends.
I express gratitude.

Dr. Edgar W. Hirshberg, PhD
came into my life
to become
my mentor in
creative writing;
a student
at age sixty-eight,
never to be forgotten.

There are three things that last forever,
faith, hope and love.
The greatest of them is love.
I Corinthians 13

The Year 2013

To the Friend Who Opened this Book,

Since I am not sitting with you enjoying a cup of tea, I wish to say thank you for sharing with me.

I was born 57 years after President Lincoln was assassinated.

The top of my trunk of memories has burst, and I am impelled to share days long gone.

May we not forget Abraham Lincoln, the "Great Emancipator"; Winston Churchill, whose voice I recall, "Never give up!"; Yitzhak Rabin, Preserver of Israel; Martin Luther King, Jr., the Overcomer; and every defender of freedom.

I gave them a place of honor at the front of this book that we may never forget the price paid for our freedom.

Proceeds from this book will be used to benefit worthy causes; administered by a man who gives of himself without measure. When I am no longer living, he will make decisions as to needs.

May God Bless you

Lest We Forget

Westward 1840

Quilts, held in work-worn hands, women in dresses made from grain sacks, who wept and walked away from babies' graves have left the written word that we may never forget.

Home-seekers; immigrants and pioneers. Missouri to Oregon, a trail of two thousand miles in covered wagons; forty adventurers. Prairie schooners they were called, pulled by oxen, patient and gentle.

What to take and what to leave; life and death decisions.

A thousand things
Tools, plows, guns
A stove, cooking pots, tin dishes
Sugar, salt, flour
Quilts and hides
Needles and thread
Nails, a child's toy
Seeds for planting

Secret tears as they said goodbye forever to treasures; never to be seen again. Farewell.

Oxen straining beneath heavy loads. Wagons creaking, cows and mules following behind, riders on prancing horses, dogs barking, running alongside.

Schooners, heavy with possessions, canvas stretched overhead for protection from the blazing sun.

Wheels falling into deep ruts crossing rivers and streams.

* * * * *

Nightfall.

Wagons circled; protection from the unseen. Campfires of buffalo chips and dry grass. Cows to be milked, repairs to damaged leather and wagons. Weary travelers lie under starry skies, remembering loved ones left behind and soft feather beds.

Some saw prairie as the Promised Land, unhitching their oxen and waving farewell to those whose vision pushed them westward.

Day after day
Burning sun
Wind blowing ceaselessly
Thunder, lightning, rain, hail

Babies birthed in covered wagons, some never to see the light of day; left to sleep beneath prairie sod.

For some the vision had dimmed. Few trees on the prairie; they built a sod house with dirt floors, oiled paper for windows. A door with leather hinges.

The buffalo, sustainer of life
Hides and food
Skins for clothes and shoes
Soap and candles from fat
Buffalo chips for heat and cooking.

Seed planting, promise of harvest
Suddenly grasshoppers, stripping every leaf

Miles down the Oregon Trail, the first cold winds of winter
Fur traders killed buffalo for hides, the meat left to rot.

Indians, whose lives depended on the buffalo,
saw the white man as his enemy,
Killing and scalping them.
Stories of pale faces living among Indians.

Survivors; dreams shattered.
Oxen, emaciated; hides cooked for soup

In the distance, a mountain
Whips crack!
Clinging to rocks, cliffs, mountain sides

Can you see them?
Standing on the summit,
Gazing at their land of dreams
Threadbare pilgrims
Tears, hidden for so long
Coursing down weathered cheeks

Calloused and scarred
Sun and wind burned
Starving, clothes worn to shreds
Courageous beyond measure
Visionaries

Adversity forges strong bonds
Pass it on!
The heritage of those we have never seen
The debt can never be reckoned

Lest we forget.

Final Journey

April 15, 1865
The guns are silent
Sixth day of peace

A small piece of metal
How could it change history?
Did the man who fashioned it know its destination?
That it would forever still the voice of Abraham Lincoln?

His black inauguration suit covered the tall, still form.
Home to the White House for the last time.

Echo of hammers; carpenters build the catafalque for the huge coffin.

Chandeliers and mirrors encased in shrouds.

Silently, one by one, mourners stopped to gaze at the man who
survived the war but fell from an assassin's bullet.

Invalid soldiers, with canes and crutches, bid farewell to their
Commander-in-Chief.

Nightfall; all is silent.

Carriages, trains and wagons
Mourners, arms circled in black crepe

Weary travelers searching for a place to rest in a
city devastated with grief.

* * * * *

April 19, 1865
Sunrise, with a cloudless sky
Last day of a final goodbye

Six white horses for his journey to the Capitol; into the rotunda
Honor guard at attention
Sound of bells and cannons

A few words
"The grass withereth and the flower thereof fadeth away."

Lincoln's son, Willie, dead three years,
was placed on the black-draped train.
Father and son together in death

Heads bowed, the funeral train moves slowly, bells tolling.

Baltimore, Harrisburg, Philadelphia, New York, Albany;
cities of mourning
Streets Lincoln has never seen receive him.
Flowers, crushed, perfume the air.
Train; patiently awaits his return

Slowly, the journey continues.
Ohio, Indiana, Illinois

Mourners, kneeling and weeping, as the train moves slowly through
villages and cities, five miles an hour

Moving toward its destination through hills and fields,
mourners wait patiently as the train passes

Chicago, a grieving city
Memories of victory

Four years from victory to tragedy
A place of honor

Once again, strong arms lift him aboard the
train for his final journey

Sunrise
Springfield, Illinois
Home among friends
Memories of 25 years; streets that had known his footsteps
Flowers and blooming trees
Signs, "Welcome Home"
Funeral dirge and roll of drums

"Old Bob," Abraham Lincoln's horse and "Fido" his dog,
left behind when he moved to the Capitol,
Followed their master in the hearse pulled by
six black horses led by a Negro
Twenty-one gun salute

Country road to Oak Ridge Cemetery
Memories, as friends and neighbors follow behind
Giant man; humorous, often sad
Dedicated servant

Along the brook to the hillside
Inside the vault; a small coffin
Abraham Lincoln is placed beside his son
The last words, his Inaugural Address
The gates of the tomb close
A journey of seventeen hundred miles
Twelve funerals

Melody of birds, sighing of the wind
Embraced by the land he loved

Winston
1874-1965

Magnificent castle of Blenheim,
320 rooms, acres of gardens
Proper setting for a child touched by destiny

Born in 1874 to Lord Randolph Churchill,
charming and unstable
His mother, Jennie, an American
beautiful and intelligent

A little boy, left in the care of a servant who loved
him without reserve

His parents – strangers
Brash and stubborn, he was sent to boarding school.
Harsh discipline, depressing atmosphere
His health broken, he was sent to Harrow, an honor institution.
Sick in body, a speech impediment
Object of humiliation and punishment

"Someday," he said.

Alone, without friends
Toy soldiers fascinated him; hours spent alone in strategy
Battles; charges and retreats
A taste of power on a toy soldier's battlefield

A tutor gave him courage.
No university for Winston

He never knew his father.
His mother, selfish and carefree

Appointment to the Queen's military
Adventure and danger
Cuba, Egypt, South Africa
A returning hero

Politics become his mistress.
Words flowed like a river.

Love entered with Clementine,
Opinionated, strong will, lust for power
Parliament, his goal
A man of action but destined for failure.
Depression became his lifetime companion,
Hidden with humor and courage.

Britain – master of the sea
Winston – First Lord of the Admiralty
Founder of the Royal Air Force
Minister of Munitions
Chancellor of the Exchequer
Enemies cries, "Not trustworthy."

Disgrace.

Hitler's star began to rise, a meteoric ascent.
Winston, a strong voice of warning
Parliament turned a deaf ear.
"Paranoid," they said.
Ridicule surrounded him.
A lone voice, warning of danger
When disaster came, he stood alone.
No one to take the reins
The world darkened as hope lay dying.

Winston, standing in the wings, answered the call.
From Number 10 Downing Street, as Prime Minister of Britain
Defiant, his words like a sharp bayonet

Germany, smashing the will to fight as Britain faltered.
Submarines lurking in dark waters.
Reality.

From political ashes rose the man of destiny.

"Victory at all cost!"
Promising only blood, sweat, toil and tears
Bloodied but not bowed

The Lion's voice carried round the world
"We shall go to the end, we shall never surrender."

The test to try men's souls
The Battle of Britain

Children sent to the country to preserve Britain's heritage.
Voice from the Reichstag offering peace
Across the channel, "We will never surrender!"
Airfield, alive with planes, young pilots in a baptism of fire

Blackouts; waves of Nazi planes
Bomb shelters, night after night
Fire raining from the sky; sirens wailing
Gas and water pipes erupting; buildings crumbling

Dark pall, hanging low
What to brighten the day?
"Old Winnie," climbing over rubble, smiling
Brisk steps, others joining him

Contempt for those who believed England would bow
Confidence flowed from him, inspiring courage.
Hope on the shoulders of an old man

V.E. Day May 5, 1945
We leave him at his finest hour.
Millions of words, written and spoken
Five years underground
Winston, a defender, he left rebuilding to others.

How short, the memory!
In peace he faded into reminiscence.
Fifty years in the House of Commons,
Serving under six monarchs
A sentimental man, shedding tears for his suffering nation

January 24, 1965
The magnificent voice still

Bells tolled as England paid homage.
320,000 mourners passed by the great statesman
in Westminster Abbey.
Through wintry streets he was carried on a gun carriage.
Royalty and many of the world's great followed to
St. Paul's Cathedral.
In a country churchyard in Bladon he lies in the soil of
the England he so nobly defended.

Yitzhak Rabin
1922-1995

He exchanged the sword for an olive branch.
The price – his life
His young hands held weapons with ease,
preserving the Holy Land for the Messiah.
Defender of Jerusalem; city of his birth
Warrior, living not far removed from the death angel
Chief of Staff, Ambassador, Prime Minister
Each mantle fit his shoulders well.
Visionary for his beloved nation

Isaiah's words, "The desert shall rejoice and blossom as the rose."
His eyes beheld the wondrous sight as perfume surrounded him.
Partaker of Israel, born anew
Star of David shouting a silent message to the world
In the planting, tares fell with the grain
bringing forth a harvest of hate.
The voice of the Lord extolling justice and judgment
Jehovah's covenant with Abraham echoing through centuries.
As he became bold in war, he was bold in peace.

Threats and strident voices
Fear of failure stronger than fear of death

The blood of Abraham courses through the veins of the man who
silenced him.
The message lives though the messenger's voice is silent.
Bitter the herbs of hate!

Final journey through rocky hills
Trod by patriarchs of long ago

Prayer for the Dead
Martyr for peace, wrapped in a white shroud,
Lowered into the earth he defended
Tributes of tears remain as stars replace flickering candles

Shalom.

The wilderness and the solitary place shall be glad for them,
and the desert shall rejoice and blossom as the rose.
Isaiah 35:1

Martin Luther King, Jr.
1925-1968

Warning against the love of money has fallen on deaf ears for
centuries.
Ships filled with dark-skinned men and women exchanged for gold
Slaves in a strange land
Grief has no color.
Decades without hope
Black arms holding white babies with love and tenderness
Tables, laden with food, planted and prepared with black hands
Generations in tiny cabins, waiting in vain for their Moses
Who determines freedom for every human?
Why will one man submit to injustice; another stand tall?
We will never understand.
Winds of change, nearly unnoticed
One voice among thousands
Courage!
Martin Luther King, Jr.
Abuse does not discourage him or control his life.
Blows and insults are no threat to dedication.
Ignored are heat and cold
Weariness and hunger.

Martin Luther King, Jr.
You stand on that fateful day, harvest of your time and labor,
Singing with joy, "We Shall Overcome."

Your enemies silenced your voice, but did not destroy your dream.

What Price?

Gettysburg 1861
Valor, wearing Blue and Gray
Gentle, peaceful slopes
Resting place of battle-weary men

Flanders 1918
"The Great War"
Scarred earth healed
White crosses, row upon row

Nuremburg 1934
Adulation for madman
Swastikas and pageantry
Bloody journey to pit of defeat

Pearl Harbor 1941
Waves lapping rusting steel
Rainbows of oil from the crypt, *Arizona*
Graveyard of battleships

Korea 1953
Armistice – painful compromise
Thirty seven tortuous months
No victory, no celebration

Vietnam
Black walls, searching eyes
Tears and flowers
The healing of a nation

Arlington
Memories etched in marble

Great and small sleep together
City of the dead

Decades of words about peace
Once again we need to hear

A tall man, slightly bent with age
Living again
The sound of plane motors, years removed
Never forgotten
Hatch open
Hurled into nothingness, human projectile

Parachute – line to life
Tightly strapped, heavily weighted
Grenades, rifle, food and water
A hundred essentials
Alone above alien soil
Puffs of smoke, steel fragments hurtling past
Perhaps bearing his name
Counting, waiting for the umbrella overhead
His mind reviewing maps and pictures
Terra firma

Normandy
Pastoral countryside
Fields and hedgerows
A few lingering blossoms
Cows grazing, milkmaids
Small villages
Terrified people, fearing retribution
Frustration of language
Night skies illumined by arsenal of war
Enemies, a stone's throw away

Digging foxholes, jumping in ditches
Comrades seen, then gone, perhaps forever
So few to vanquish thousands
God alone knew the nearness of death
Miracles which can never be explained
Sounds of battle diminish into silence.

To the young who do not remember or have not heard
Pursue peace, it is elusive.

Contents

Let It Unfold

A very wise man, King Solomon, said, "A word fitly spoken is like apples of gold in a picture of silver."

Some words fade quickly, remembered no more. Others remain forever in our memory.

I heard these words in 1972, spoken by a young man who will never know how many places I have scattered them.

He was very impatient, always wanting answers, now, if not sooner.

He was invited to visit an older minister in California.

When he arrived it was apparent to the older man that his visitor was in need of patience.

In his wisdom he waited for circumstances rather than words alone.

One morning they walked together in the rose garden.

The older man took his pocket knife, cut a rosebud and gave it to the young man with the words, "Unfold it."

His visitor replied, "I can't."

The minister repeated, "Unfold it."

The young man carefully pulled on the petals. They fell in pieces in his hand.

The minister cut a beautiful rose in full bloom. He said, "God unfolded this. It took a long time; cold wind, hot sun, rain and fertilizer. When God finished, it is beautiful with a lovely fragrance. We must allow our lives to unfold in God's time."

Sometimes words are more precious than silver or gold.

The Writer

Books I borrowed as a child
Led me down a path adventuresome.
Words lived in an orderly array.
Some looked familiar;
I had met them many times before.
Others were strangers I had never seen.
To those I knew I said, "Come, sit with me."
The strangers said, "We saw you once before.
You ran past, we didn't have time to say 'hello'."
They introduced themselves and we became
companions and warm friends.
Seasons passed, I closed the gate on youth
And journeyed through another door.
Working days and baby's hands held me fast.
Inside, words tumbled in profusion,
Struggling to be free.
One day, the sound of laughter bid me pause.
Not often did I listen to insistent voices calling me.
I remembered Pandora's box.
Tantalized by curiosity, I stood before a door,
Slowly I turned the key and opened it a bit
Lest confusion reign.
Words danced out, flinging wide the door.
They had been in prison for so long.
Tall and short
Vibrant, austere, radiant, hostile
Beguiling, scornful, vivacious, elusive
A line so long I couldn't see the end.
"We have no place to live," they cried.
As I watched they become people I love,
Places I have gone,
Beauty I have seen.

"I cannot turn them out," I said.
I must find space somewhere.
To some, I promise they could visit me another day;
I'd call them when I had the time.
I made room for those who were my oldest friends.
Lately, I've had visitors I've never met;
In fact, sometimes I do not know their names.
I must ask Mr. Webster if he knows who they are.
No doubt, someday, they too shall live with me.

The delight of a book has not grown old to me.
Summertime, as a child, I walked
To the library every week, about a mile, by myself.
I read as I walked the country road.
There weren't many cars and their speed was low.
One elderly lady drove a horse and buggy;
The horse, like his owner, was an old-timer.
If we were alone, occasionally she invited a child to ride.
I was the eldest of eight children so I had responsibilities;
However, I lived so many lifetimes from pages of books.

Immigrant

What magic words stirred visions of a far-off land?
Perhaps it may have been the weariness of turning sod year after year.
The Sabbath, a day of rest
Sitting on an old wood pew
Gazing through the window at gravestones in the church yard
Your name engraved from generations past.
Why are you restless when those gone before remained content to die
upon this land?

A stranger passed your way one summer day.
He told of cities reaching for the sky; fortunes could be made.
Pictures, drawn with words, that time did not erase.
Oblivious to arms holding you close
Dreams more possessive than flesh and blood
Tearful promises for your return
A well-worn trunk, talisman for lonely days

Long and winding road, ever toward the sea
The final hill, the harbor and beyond, where water meets the sky

Unknown, mysterious, so many fathoms deep and miles across
Tiller of the soil
You must place your life in hands that never knew a plow;
Those who trust in compass, sea charts, constellations of stars
Daydreams become reality at the rolling of
the deck beneath your feet.
"Farewell, land that nurtured me, farewell."

Blazing sun, soft sea breezes.
Clouds, drifting gently
Slowly, the breeze becomes a gale.
Waves pitch the ship.

Decks awash, timbers creaking
Dark, scudding clouds
No sun, moon or stars
Gray misery
Alone
Does fate decree Neptune's shroud?
With anguished heart, you are consumed with haunting memories.

A ray of sun through murky sky
Tumultuous seas return to gentle swells
Day after day, you hover between despair and hope.
Is that the long awaited cry, "Land Ho!"?

The gangplank is your ticket to a bright, new world.
Pursue your dreams!
We leave you to plow new furrows in a vibrant land.
You are the adventurer we long to be.
History will portray seasons of your life.
Godspeed!

Family

We did not choose each other.
One by one we came,
Green eyes and brown.
No question, "Is there room?"
More patches on the clothes
More children in a bed
Scary doesn't seem so bad with someone near.
Secrets, whispered and forgotten long ago
We dreamed of treasures we never found.
More to play hide and seek
More taking turns
Busy hands to pull weeds
Climbing trees and swinging from branches
Barefoot, we ran on cinder roads.
Flying kites on windy days
Homemade whistles, loud and shrill
Lying in the grass watching clouds drifting by
Someone to talk with as we walked to school
The ice man, with horse and wagon, clip-clopping down
the country road
We had no money to pay for ice.
Small pieces he reserved for us,
Ambrosia on a summer day.
Wrapped in newsprint we licked them to oblivion.
Steam calliope, paintings gleaming
Like the Pied Piper of ancient days, the melodies enchanted us.
The circus was in town.
Playing on the porch on rainy days
Hopscotch on the sidewalk squares
Jump the rope – one, two, you are out.
When neighbors came we listened to their wondrous tales.
In our minds we lived it all again.

Around the table, dividing what we had
"Mom, he has the biggest piece," we said.
Somehow we learned that sharing is part of the game.

Strange that togetherness produced no clones.
No cookie-cutter kids are in this group.
Some read, some played, some pounded nails.
Time has not stood still.
A slower pace than in years gone by
No trees to climb, no kites to fly.
Some of the little boy and girl remains.
Sometimes I look at you and see a bit of me.
With pride I note what you have done.

Words of love we felt but seldom spoke.
Let me tell you now when you can hear.
You shall always be a part of me.
We have traveled different roads and gone our separate ways.
We meet, soon to say goodbye
May the memories we share help us to remember.
Love has no measure or bounds.

With love,
To my family

The Gate

The haunting strains of Stephen Foster's "Old Kentucky Home" fill
me with nostalgia.
A child's view of slavery from words in a song book

Plaintive refrain, nearly forgotten –
The final notes linger.
Thoughts and pictures hold me captive –
A small school room, song book in my hands.
Words I never understood.
I sang about an old Kentucky home.
Kentucky was a map in a book.
I knew about sunshine and summer,
Flowers in a meadow, birds singing.
I could understand that.
When hard times came, slaves bid goodbye to the little cabin.
No more they hunted or sat on a bench in the moonlight, singing.
Shadows over the heart brought sorrow.
Why did they carry heavy loads with bent backs?
With bowed heads they parted from each other.

Whatever happened in my life, I never left home.
Injustice was a foreign word.
I don't remember when I understood.
Love and hate surround me.
I built a strong wall –
One gate, inscribed
"Only love may enter and remain."

Frontiersman

One man spends his life from birth to death –
One plot of earth
Content to hunt and fish,
Clearing land to plant cotton and corn.

Another stands beside a forge,
Working bellows, anvil and hammer.
His life spent shaping horseshoes.

Boatloads of immigrants
Tavern keepers, tradesmen, gunsmiths
Fierce fighters, recruited to fight Indians
Horse thieves
Wilderness justice – hanging

Now and then is born a man,
Restless and adventuresome.
Reading signs the unwary never see.
Tracks and animal prints
Following a trace –
Trail blazed by wild creatures to a cold bubbling spring or salt lick
Precious salt for preserving meat
Roots and herbs for the sick and wounded
Tanning leather for buckskin
Hides for trading

With marriage, the building of a cabin
Promises to forsake the life of a wanderer
Promises he couldn't keep
Wanderlust, an incurable malady

Clearing, planting, then farewell
Horse and saddle
Rifle, powder and lead
Knife, blanket, dried venison

Riding through forest, hills and marshes
Sun, rain, sleet and snow
Sleeping under stars
Moss and branches for his bed
Freedom, like heady wine

Sometimes a stranger's cabin
Settlers, hungry for news
Trading food and lodging for words of home
Goodbye

Eyes and ears attuned to danger –
Footprints
Smoke
The neighing of a horse

Wading rivers, covering tracks
Scars for life from wild animals
Strong, sinewy muscles, his defense

Indians, friends and foes

Weeks and miles behind
Young woman in a cabin
Lonely, struggling to exist
Birth a child, alone
Tending a garden
Milking the cow, feeding animals, chopping wood
A cooking pot, hanging in the fireplace

Frightening noises
Her rifle ready to fire

Curious Indians
Sharing precious handfuls of food

Singing lullabies as she sews
Her greatest enemy – loneliness
Wild creatures for friends
Sometimes a wagon on the trail
Joy of new faces
Laughter and tears
A few hours of remembering and forgetting

Galloping horse approaching
A woodsman, alone
Clothes, worn and faded
Beloved face, tired but happy
Hardships forgotten
Homecoming

Many accounts have been written concerning the loss, suffering and tears of the early settlers and pioneers. My grandfather came to the United States from Switzerland. My grandmother came alone at age 16. They married in Illinois and had eighteen children. No English, only French until the children attended school and learned English from their teachers. How sad that I have no written accounts!

No one living. -B.P.

A Country Boy's Sunday

Sunday mornin' summer time
It's just a-gittin' light.
I smell the coffee brewin'
Ma baked a pie last night.

I forgot it's Sunday mornin'.
Sunday clothes hangin' on the chair.
There's the church bell ringin'
I washed my face and combed my hair.

Pa's sittin' at the table.
Ma put the skillit on the range.
Bacon, eggs and biskits
Some things don't seem to change.

"Pa, go kill a chicken,
I'll put it on to cook.
See if there's eggs in the hen house.
I got no time to look.

"Bring taters from the cellar, son.
Pump a pail of water, too.
Hurry, the church bell's ringin' –
Too many things to do!"

An hour and a half's not long at all
When at the creek a-fishin
These old pews are hard as nails
When I'm sittin' and a-listenin'.

Folks stand 'round a-talkin'.
Aw! Paw invited Uncle Bill.

He shoulda killed two chickens.
It takes one fer Uncle Bill.

The porch is cool and shady.
Dinner over, dishes done
Ma and Pa, rockin' on the porch
Is this what they call fun?

When I grow up to be a man,
I'm not a-livin' here.
No pumpin' water, carryin' wood
I'll come to visit once a year.

I'll own a big house, built of brick
Blue carpet on the floor
Bright lights through every window.
Maybe – I'll build a porch.

People, born and raised in the South
intrigue me. Southern people I have known
are interesting. They are portrayed as relaxed
and nonchalant. When in the South I have enjoyed
many types of personalities.
–B.P.

September's Child

"When, Mommy?
How many days?"
One, two, three little fingers
Three seems forever
at five years young.
Lunch box
shiny and red
awaiting an apple
a peanut butter sandwich
Clothes,
replicas of a
thousand little girls
Pencil and paper,
clutched in little fingers
that knew how
to print her name.
She skipped away,
eyes bright and happy.
My misty eyes
looked back
so long ago and saw
another little girl.
I smiled and dried my tears.

Passage

time between
childhood
and maturity,
carefree days
and
reality
seemed but
a moment,
the
rocking chair
a memory,
she
went to sleep
a child
filled with laughter,
awakened
to an unfamiliar world,
thirteen,
no more
the
wind-blown hair,
grass stains
and sunburned nose,
passé,
she stood
beside me –
a
shadow
passed
between,
with tears
I saw she was
thirteen going on twenty

Chasing the Wind
(Lest We Forget)

Little is what it seems.
The future hidden except from the eyes of God
What fuel to feed the fire?

Wise man.

Knowledge unsurpassed
Wealth beyond measure
Vineyards and gardens
Rare jewels
Servants
Sumptuous feasts
Sensual harem
Earthly paradise
Whatever his heart desires

The song of fools!

Never enough

One day, all will be forgotten.
We pass through life as a shadow –
To dust we return, both fool and wise man.

Hidden in the heart, knowledge of eternity
The light of heaven dispels the darkness;
If we so desire

-King Solomon

Once Again

I remember dreams, but they never really lived,
Like rose petals in the heat of summer.
Dying too soon, with only an elusive fragrance remaining

Pursuing tomorrow, life spun a web
Surrounding me, an invisible thread
From another time and place,
Perfume lingers in remembrance from roses past.

Lost years, bright with dreams
I gather them from where they have fallen.

I looked up.
The sky was blue, and the birds were singing.

Sometimes, in the midst of a difficult time
in our lives, we become overwhelmed,
forgetting all the wonderful times.
At those times I have tried to recall
something that had blessed me
in a special way. Have a wonderful day!
B.P.

Home before Dark

Crushed stone beneath my feet
Many times I've walked this road,
gathering wild roses along the way.
Through the trees, the old house
weathered to silver
Porch, leaning on the house for support
Memories of churning thick cream to butter
How many years since voices filled
the rooms, and children tumbled in the grass!
Motionless I stand as past summer days
wash over me.

Melody of bird songs
Music of the small stream wending its way to the swamp.
I remember trudging up the hill, bare feet
burning from summer sand.
The cow, following along behind, chain around her neck
To be staked in thick clover, returning at
noon to the stream for water

Mother's voice, "Come home before dark!"
Roaming in fields, collecting treasures
Harvest of a summer afternoon
Childhood days, not measured by the ticking of a clock
Swiftly the curtain of night falls.
Running, as the sun's last rays disappear

There it is!
A light in the window.
Lamp; glass polished, flame brightly gleaming
Mother never forgets.

I stand alone at sundown as shadows appear.
Evening mist rises above the stream.
Moonbeams through a veil of clouds
Someone who loves me remembers the light,
That I might not stumble in the darkness.

Closing Chapter

hope
so long deferred
whispering
a melody
so gentle
I must
hear it
again
to believe,
for I
have waited
so long,
my anguished heart
not letting go
but fearful;
not daring to hope
the storm
would pass
and peace spread its mantle
over me

Intangibles

how can a lifetime
yield so little
of this world's goods?
a long life
given to love
and sacrifices,
she said, "farewell"
and closed her eyes.
we remain
to put away
the meager things
she left behind;
an old trunk
bought to hold
her few possessions.
when she spoke
her wedding vows,
moved from
place to place
with added scars
as time passed by.
her wedding dress
that did not look
like a bridal gown,
it was the best she had.
she cut her long,
shining hair
and packed it in
a little box.
we caught a glimpse

of someone young
we only knew as
"Mom."

photographs
of happy days
when those we loved
were gathered near.
letters,
tied with ribbon
from sons
who marched to war.
cards,
far-off places
she never saw.
pieces of clay,
brightly painted,
molded by childish hands
that knew
just what they were.
worn dresses,
with hems let down,
she loved
the old ways best.
new shoes
in a box,
shoes she wore
were like
old friends.
dishes,
cracked but loved,
that she could never
throw away.

pans with handles missing,
"I like the old ones best."
pictures
painted years ago,
faded now.

we,
who are part of her,
cherish treasures
that she left.
nothing
we hold in our hands,
words
remembered
that we share.
patience
never-ending
as we now look back.
compassion
reaching out
to those in need.
when we were grown,
we brought her gifts
she never used.
she
always found someone
who had much less.
the worth of millionaires
can never buy
riches
that are ours.
words
like jewels

hidden away
where thieves
cannot break in
to steal.

Dedicated to our mother Cora Petersen Eggen,
With Love
1898-1985

Destiny

He wears custom suits and ties;
his office impressive, walnut and brass
Desk piled high with large accounts,
secure within what the future holds
Fortune abounding, horizon afar
Decisions today, wealth tomorrow
Measuring success with silver and gold

The One who rules heaven had no home,
walking dusty roads with a faithful few.
Days on hillsides and seashores
His kingdom, the poor and forgotten
the defeated lay in their graves.
Hope, comfort when lonely
The future, more precious than treasures

Sunrise and sunset
Lifetime of decisions

Unfamiliar voice
"Follow me."

You, who love security
When mountains tremble
and Earth is shaken
Have you invested wisely?

You, alone, have the answer.

Vineyard

Cold winter winds linger into March.
The old man, with pruning shears, walks between the rows.

Grapevines
Remnants of last year's harvest
Hands, numb with cold, reach out.
Relentlessly, they cut away.
Four small vines tied securely to the wire.
So little left to grow
Decades of judgment spare fruitful vines.
A mountain of lifeless wood crackles as it blazes.

Slowly it fades into gray ash.
Snow, rain, sunshine, dew
Mingled with time
September
Aging hands cradle the luscious grapes.
Reward of pruning and patience

Oh, that I so easily sever from my life dead wood.
Torch it to wisps of smoke.

Butterfly

ethereal creature,
where do you hide
as the storm
flings its fury?
moments ago
a nomad
suddenly gone
somewhere
with folded wings
awaiting prisms of
sunlight
to feast
upon
nectar from
sun-kissed blossoms

Do You Know?

Some things
I'll
never understand.
It isn't
that
I haven't tried.
I know why
God
made birds and bees.
Why the
bedbugs and fleas?

Infinity

Hopes and fears, concealed from eyes of strangers
Shadows of secret places
No one lives immune from anguish.
One moment, giddy with life
The next, a tempestuous abyss
Life calls.
The ascent is long and steep,
a perilous journey.
The ultimate goal –
that death becomes a refuge.
Sorrow for those void of understanding,
who never really lived.

Loneliness

Many voices, few who listen
A line here and there
Palace or hovel
Loneliness, like ashes cold upon a hearth
Soon May becomes December.

Listen
before the draught of age
dries the spring

Few blossoms flourish in the arid land.
Fertile the garden watered by a
serene and tender heart.

The Child in Me

Kaleidoscope of childhood, long ago
Precious reflections
Days and years become a whimsical dream.
Woven ribbons of love's recurring themes

Grown-up five I carefully printed my name.
Page, bright and clean, no mistakes
Summer days; sunshine and showers
Symphony of life, laughter and tears
Secret places where fairies hide
High in a ~~wing~~, swing, soaring to touch a cloud
Longing to be a bird in flight
Earthbound was I.

School bells ringing goodbye to summer
Birds departing to follow the sun
Brown leaves whisper farewell sighs.
Snowflakes dancing, blustery winds
Myriad footprints on pristine snow
A battered old sled, we flew down the hill.
Waving, shouting at friends below
Helter, skelter we tumbled like Jack and Jill.

Silence

Miles in distance and years
Children, grown and scattered

Those who love me remember the child in me.

Psalm 56:8

Why are you dismayed, my soul?
This is not your promised land.
Silent tears where no one sees,
recorded in your Book beside my name.
I do not weep in vain.
You told me that I might understand.

Alone, you wept that you might overcome death's shadow.
How may I comprehend unselfish love
that held you on the cross?
Forgiving those who hated you
Ultimate love
All I have to offer is myself.

A day of hope dawns at life's darkest hour.

Dear Jesus, Help me to remember
that the day will come when
you shall dry the tears from my eyes.
Revelation 21:4
B.P.

Mountain Handyman

Bill was his name.
His last name no one knew, or where he was born.
No stranger to mountain people
Tall, spare man, bronzed, weathered face.
Gnarled, calloused hands
He had no home.
Not much more than the clothes on his back;
Sturdy, worn boots
Treasures never seen in a battered suitcase
Work to be done? He'd stay awhile.
A week here, a month there
Piles of wood split, corn shelled
Cutting trees, clearing land
Hitching the mule to the plow
Piling rocks for a fence
Shaping shingles for the roof

At dusk lamps are lit.
A chair by the fire; cornbread and beans
Quilt and pillow in the loft
Falling asleep to the hooting of an owl
First rays of morning light
Time to be on his way
Trudging mountain roads until an arm in a faded shirt beckons
"Help wanted"
Gray hair and bent back
Bill moved more slowly with the years.

When he died they laid him to rest with their kinfolks in the valley.
In every cabin and field, memories of Bill remain.

My World

I saw her face, a smile in place
Proper word; perfection
Ladies curtsies, spotless gloves
Jeweled crown and palace

Would I desire to be a queen?

No, a thousand times

Protocol from birth to death
Surrounded, yet alone

I am free to roam if I so choose.
I walk in rain with no umbrella.
Fruit from the tree in my garden
Barefoot, sit upon the grass
Watch the clouds drift past

Concert by a feathered choir
Admission price, a cup of seeds

Worlds removed from pomp and ceremony

Indictment

We search in vain for men with answers,
Listening to voices with little meaning.
Charisma blinds us and stops our ears.
The greatest man who walked the earth taught us to embrace peace.

He spoke softly;
Quiet voices are seldom heard.
Multitudes listened and left.
We ask for strident voices with easy answers.
Centuries have taught us little.
Who is our enemy?
We don't know him when we see him.
Yesterday he was our friend.
Greed arms friends and foes alike.
We are pierced with shrapnel our hands have made.

Brother against brother
Abel's blood pollutes the ground;
It has never been cleansed.
We cover the bloodstains and try to forget where they are.
Those who live by the sword shall die by the sword.
Oh, that we could beat swords into plowshares.
We are not willing to pay the price.

The light is dim.
In the shadows, feet of clay

Heartprints

No words in ink to bridge the years;
No pictures of halcyon yesterdays, another time and place.

Concert in the park
Melody filtering through emerald leaves
The touch of loving hands
Nostalgia reflected in shadowed eyes.
Serene interlude before winds of change blow harsh and cold.
Hidden, where ink does not grow dim or pictures fade;
Heartprints: when eyes are dim with tears and the
taste of life is bitter.

Never to Be Forgotten
A Summer Concert

Swiss ancestors are in my heritage.
A Swiss cousin, who spoke no English came to visit.
My aunts, age 70 and 80, recalled a little French from childhood.
On a summer evening we sat on the grass for a summer symphony
concert
in Bronson Park, Kalamazoo, Michigan.
Imagine my Swiss cousin's excitement when the orchestra began to
play
"The William Tell Overture." He laughed and waved his arms
as he expressed his delight in French.
We saw our heritage with new eyes during his visit.

Consolation
(Jeremiah 18:1-4)

Remember the times you heard, "Don't cry"?
Memory has vanished in mist of long ago.
Tears hide until we need them.
They are only a moment away.

Tears of joy, enhanced with sharing
Pain of the soul not often seen
We weep alone with failure and sorrow.

There is one place of beginning again.
On the potter's wheel, clay that was marred was shaped once more.
Another vessel, finer than before;
Something lovely from failure.

Michelangelo's masterpiece *David* was sculpted from imperfect marble.
Who remembers the names of sculptors who began with perfect stone?
Michelangelo struggled to fashion David from that which was flawed.

Make something beautiful of the ordinary.

When I visited Italy I stood before
the famous statue of David as
the professor explained that Michelangelo
had arrived late to compete for sculpting.
The choice pieces of marble were taken.
He had to carefully position one of
David's hands to fit the only remaining
piece of marble.
B.P.

Disenchantment
(H.R.H. Princess of Wales)

The magic is gone, once-upon-a-time days.

Searching for the joy of love,
Captivated by a prince

Waiting in the timeless cathedral
The great organ resounding against ancient walls

Pageantry of centuries
Poised, the flawless face, radiant
Capturing hearts with elegance
Lavish praise fell round about her.
Golden splendor shared with the world
Diamond tiara
Royal coach

So few catch a falling star.

Sacred vows exchanged, soon to become broken promises.
Clinging cobwebs of memory
Heartbreak knocks at palace doors
The veneer stripped away
Orchestration of betrayal, endless melody
A locked door with no key

Castle in the clouds lost in the mist
The magic is gone.

Princess without a kingdom

Home

Walls surround me, so familiar.
Why am I sometimes a stranger here?
Decades removed from childhood –
Mother, my security
No question; a loving welcome.

Windows of home, dark; the door closed.
No more the warm kitchen; crusty bread.
What compares with belonging?

With tenderness I remember work-worn hands;
Mute reminder of the price of caring.
Her essence remains ever with me.

Glowing marigolds on cloudy days.
Morning glories greeting the sun

I have lost the way to the road which led home.
Come, share a bowl of soup with me.

*From birth to death, we rarely remain
in the same place. At times, we return
to disappointment, and we must live
with happy memories of times past.*
-B.P.

Pioneers

It stood in the clearing;
Logs once so strong, weathered by countless storms.
Could I turn back the hands of time!

Newly-wed
Eyes filled with stars
"We will build it here," he said.
"Sheltered in the trees.
The roof strong, windows for sunshine."
She smiled.
"I can see you working in the field.
I will be safe here."

No tree yet fallen
Dreams are made of so little.
Summer past
Snow piled on the roof
Silver rain on a day in spring
Moonbeams on a soft, summer night

So swiftly down the path of life
The ring of the ax, now silent
Hands that tilled the soil and rocked the cradle are still.
Somewhere, courage survives, nurtured with love and trust.

Afternoon in a Mountain Meadow

The hillside glowed with scattered flowers.
Wild narcissus, cultivated by God
Dark green pines, stately and tall
Mountain lake, far below, calm and smooth
Reflecting blue of springtime skies
Mountains; sentinels, surround the lake

A tiny woman, bent, hands outstretched,
Gently lifting blossoms from the grass.
Simple pleasure; picking flowers in the sun
The habit she wore spoke of a separated life.
Slowly she stood, smiling at me.
Time had etched her face.

I pictured her as once she must have looked;
Cheeks rosy with youth, stepping lightly.
The convent gate closed behind her,
Dreams exchanged for duty.
Kneeling on cold stone floors by candlelight
Faithfully offering prayers for those she loved.

Disciplined hands remember days when
As a child, she filled her mother's hands with flowers.

At nightfall in her simple room,
Behind stone walls, narcissus blossomed as she slept.

Memories of an afternoon in a meadow of
flowers in Switzerland.
B.P.

Choices

Manicured lawns that touch the bay.
Mansions, soft lights gleaming
Slender woman, precious pearls
Designer dresses, wrapped in furs
Exotic perfume from distant lands

Millionaires with furrowed brows
Diamond rings and custom suits
Young men driving their Mercedes
Private yachts with well-stocked bars
Toys for grown-up girls and boys.

Success?
Fickle mistress

Once, a dream
You've done it all.
What price did you pay?
"Could we go to the park today?"
"Daddy, sail my boat with me."
Mommy, let's make cookies."

Do you remember questioning eyes?
Waiting for answers that never come
A little longer, next year you'll have it made.

A Simple Goodbye

They walk past, hesitant and quiet.
Some reach to touch her hand.
Her hair, carefully brushed
They remember her in modest disarray.
Wisps of hair, flour on her dress,
As she baked cookies, hung washing on the line.

Her hands, quiet now
Not as they recalled –
Peeling potatoes, kneading bread
The sparkle in her sea-green eyes
No longer seen.

Pick her a bouquet from the fields –
Wild roses and daisies.
Dresses she wore were simple,
Soft from washing and gentle breezes.
Let her goodbye dress be one she loved.

Heritage

Silent, her beloved voice
Her words etched in my heart.
I've spoken them to those I love.
Time cannot erase my mother.

Death

"Hold me," she said.
This little one, three years young,
Weary of her world of make believe.
I held her gently; her brightness faded.
What trust that she could sleep in peace!
Someday, I shall say to Him,
"Hold me," and I shall close my eyes and rest.

Memorial

They dropped white roses where his ship went down at sea.
He never knew, for he was gone;
No one knew where.
Tears fell on waves as blossoms disappeared.
Oh, that they had given him flowers when he could see.

Wishes

I wish . . .
How often I have said those words.
Time for wishing now is past.
As I look upon your face, I think of all the wasted years.
Time for love at last.

Preview

I know Him as my Father, the friend who shares my
deepest thoughts and loves me.
One day I read His Book.
It told me He created Heaven and Earth.
I thought, "No wonder I like things beautiful."
He must have loved creating beauty.
He made me just a bit like Him that I could share the joy He knew.
He made flowers grow.
He sees me choose those I love the most.
He must have smiled when He thought of me,
the pleasure that He gave.
What lovely berries, fruit trees too.
He knows I like variety.
Before the fruit appears, blossoms fill the air with perfume sweet,
Enfolding me like a silken gown.
I love the sunshine on my face.
When the day is through, the moon sails overhead
with an entourage of stars;
A glimpse of worlds beyond.
When I read in His book, He has a better place for me,
There is no doubt, for I have tasted Heaven on Earth.

Time Lost

A day in springtime
Blossoms offering fragrance rare
I longed for just one rose.

A table for two
No smiles or happy talk
The food like sawdust in my mouth

I wore a dress with flowers and lace,
When you glanced my way, just another dress
You never saw the little girl inside.

We strolled along the avenue,
Shoppe windows agleam, treasures myriad.
You passed them by and never saw the longing in my eyes.

You lost me long ago.

Teardrops for what might have been.

Sometimes "first love" is wonderful, remaining a lifetime; not often.
Maturity comes with time, living and learning.
B.P.

No Ordinary Day

It was an ordinary day.
No different than so many days before.
The same sun woke my sleepy eyes to say, "Hello."
Birds that sang had sung to me before.
Breezes drifting past my face reached out and touched me like a
friend.
It was an ordinary day.

I walked along, my mind upon a thousand things.
It was an ordinary day.
Your "hello" disturbed my reverie.
Prince Charming doesn't meet you on an ordinary day.
My heart said "yes," my mind said "no."
I answered not at all.
You smiled at me.

This morning as the sun arose,
Someone had polished it like gold.

When you read this, I hope you recall a special day in your life.
Live it again in your memory.
B.P.

The Blue Dress

Once upon a time
I bought a dress.
Blue it was;
Blue as the summer sky.
Mine alone
No hand-me-down
My first new dress
Soft to touch
Fit for a princess
So I thought.

Understanding came with time.
I didn't know
Happiness is not a dress.
Nothing you own or hold
Strange
I don't remember where it disappeared.
Strawberry ice cream stains
Someone else's hand-me-down

Hats

Where did it all begin?
It's really hard to say.
With a tiny baby bonnet,
A ruffle round her face

As she grew she loved long curls,
A frilly, flowery dress.
"I don't want to wear a hat, Mom.
It will make my hair a mess."

Thirteen came around so soon.
Where had her childhood gone?
She longs to look sixteen
With heels and long skirts on.

One day when window shopping
She saw a wondrous sight.
A hat with flowers and ribbons;
Her common sense took flight.

That was the beginning
Of a lifetime filled with hats –
Every style and color.
Hats, hats, hats, hats, hats.

Hats for winter's icy blast
Hats of springtime flowers
Hats for summer sunshine
Hats for autumn's hours

If life hands you a bad hair day,
Don't you fret and sigh.
Toss a hat upon your head,
Don't sit home and cry.

I've heard so many women say,
"I wish that I could wear a hat,
I can't find one just right for me."
Don't give up like that!

Take your best friend with you,
Walk bravely through the door,
Try every style and color
Displayed inside the store.

I should warn you, it's addictive.
There's something about a hat
That lifts a woman's spirit.
There is something about a hat.

*Nearly forgotten, the days of women
wearing hats and gloves. In my box of
memories, long gloves of many colors.
Ladies, both young and old, did not shop
without wearing them. There were shops
that sold only hats. Hats worn at
the Kentucky Derby will give you
a glimpse of the long lost past.*
B.P.

Less than Perfect

The last cold wind blows south.
When I see packs of seeds something stirs within.
Reality says no farmer ever painted those pictures.
Forgotten are backaches, dirty feet and bugs.
Perfect pickles and corn
Melons, tomatoes and beans
Pickles from my garden are crooked, with warts.
Tomatoes wilt.
Ears of corn I grow are no relatives of pictures on seed packages.
Worms don't seem to care the ears are small.
Bugs who eat holes in my beans multiply by hundreds.
I feed them poison every week.
Since they don't read, they don't understand they should die.
The only reason the melons remain, the bugs don't like them.
They are not sweet enough.
They drilled a hole in every one.

I counted the cost.
Fertilizer, insecticide, and liniment
I counted the beans.
Each one cost a nickel.

Next year I'll only plant flowers.
Come to think of it, my flowers don't look like the pictures either.

Oasis

Shadows lengthen.
Life propels me swiftly through the labyrinth of time.
This day shall never live again.
Reflection bids me linger here.
Once I ran so quickly past;
Many things I never saw.
Maturity has granted me another pair of eyes.

Once I scattered words like seeds.
Now I stop to pick them up, savor them like honey in my mouth.
Bird songs, heavenly melodies
Flowers cascading on the garden wall;
Whimsical, dancing in the breeze.
Remembering times past,
I return to loved ones, long forgotten.
Holding this day near, reluctant to let it go
Oasis in a jaded world.

Hope

Lost in sorrow, words fade in grief.
Love crosses the valley with a tender touch.
One day when time has dried your tears,
From the shadows of darkness will appear
Remembrances to be cherished a lifetime.

Today

When we were young, money scarce
We had patches on our clothes.
Mama did her very best
That patches did not show.

How times have changed!
Today, when clothes are new,
Patches worn are on display.

Johnny Appleseed

September 1774 –
The state of Massachusetts
A baby boy was born into the Chapman family.
They named him John.

Revolutionary War –
His father became a soldier, his mother and brother died;
Another mother when Johnny was six.

Where does a young man escape midst the clatter of ten children?
The woods and meadowlands became his home and refuge.

The Allegheny Mountains –
A gentle, quiet lad; his friends were birds and animals.
Berries, fruits and nuts sustained him.
Wild creatures, his friends; too precious for food

Apples, shiny and red –
From cider presses Johnny acquired apple pulp.
A woodchopper, he carried bags of pulp, planting seeds.
Pioneers became his friends.
"Johnny Appleseed" they called him.
In 1800, two canoes tied together, he drifted down the Ohio River
planting orchards.
He trimmed trees, visited Indians who were his friends.

Moving westward –
Johnny's knowledge of seeds and herbs earned him the name
"medicine man."

Sleeping under the stars,
Stretching a hammock high in the trees
Ragged clothes made of coffee sacks
Barefoot, pan for a hat

When settlers came, they bought his orchards.
Little or no money, they traded old clothes or promises to pay.
Children delighted in Johnny's Bible stories.

War of 1812 –
Peaceful life disrupted.
British incited Indians to battle.
His friends at war, Johnny grieved.

Westward Indiana –
A lifetime of planting and sharing

At seventy, a victim of storms
Pneumonia took his life.

Apple blossoms in spring,
Crisp apples in autumn recall memories of a free spirit;
A wanderer with a bag of apple seeds.

When Mama Baked Bread

I've eaten bread so many years,
So many places in the world.
By candle light, on ocean waves,
On linen cloths with silver's gleam,
In a bus and on a train,
Through clouds high above the earth,
Flying swiftly in a plane,
In mountain meadows beside a stream.
As I remember by-gone days,
Nothing ever will compare
With bread that Mama made.
"This is the last loaf," Mama said.
"I guess I'd better bake some bread."
She sang a cheery little tune.
Something from her childhood days,
A certain bowl she always used.
As if some flavor to impart
Some of this, a little of that,
Ritual of the practiced eye,
She kneaded it with work-worn hands.
They understood how it should feel.
She went about her countless tasks,
Time to put it in the pans
Let it rise again.
The old wood range with blackened face,
Standing ready to exchange
Some sticks of wood for crusty loaves.

As I make my bread today,
Mixing it with stainless steel,
I long to hear her little song,
Taste again the bread that Mama made.

Serenity

The earth belongs to God.
We borrow it until we say "Farewell."

I sought a haven for life's fleeting days,
So rare a place that speaks of peace.
My heart sang when I saw the trees,
Giant umbrellas, they o'erspread the land.
How many seasons they have stood, stalwart and strong,
Shimmering heat or moonlight's silver glow.
Gently they rock cradles of little birds,
Quiet rustle of leaves, their lullaby.

Could it be this grove would welcome me?

I borrowed it from God to write my final page.
When I am battered by life's storms,
Broken, bruised and torn,
I stand among these patriarchs,
Old, unbowed.

Night winds softly playing midnight music
Enfolded in His loving arms.
Once again, that quiet assurance,
The earth and all therein belongs to God.

The Awakening

Our world
Great upheaval with millions striving to find direction.
To you, who struggle for freedom

Living in a world I do not understand, a pilgrim and a stranger.
Isolation is my cocoon.
No risk from hostile wounds, secure within walls of solitude.
Insulated from battle sounds of life

Somewhere, a secret longing to be free
A thirst to live that cries
"Reach out; place your fingers on the pulse of life."
Instinctively, I pull my cloak of safety near,
Specter of my solitary world.
Tenuously, I place my hand upon the door.
Cautiously, I gaze upon a Kingdom, almost unknown.
A taste of freedom; euphoria to the soul
Like rays of sun that stir the sleeping earth in spring
Midst cacophony of war, shadow of the dove of peace

World!
Give me space to stand and light to see.
I've lived in shadows for so long,
Tonight, I looked up and saw the stars.

Homecoming

Johnny came home yesterday.
Drums rolled, flags waved in the breeze.

"How brave he was!"
"A hero," someone said.
Speeches they made described a stranger I never knew.
I remember well a little boy who stole apples from my tree –
To sell, to buy a puppy dog.
He let my cows out through the gate.
My tools were left forgotten in the rain.
They never were the same again.
It seems a little while ago we stood together – Fourth of July.
Freckled-faced young lad with mischief in his eyes
He loved parades, the roll of drums;
Clapped his little hands to see the soldiers marching past.

Heroes are made of little boys, grown up.

I'm sorry, Johnny.
I wish you could have heard the drums.
They never sounded better, son.
The flags were flying just for you.

Seasons of Life

Spring –
Promise of life
Warmth of sun
To flowers sleeping
What measure for our days?
Time to smile, time to cry
Time to gaze with wonder
Traveler on an unfamiliar path

Summer –
Stream of life
Ruffled waters in a placid current
Raging cataract midst the storm
How to navigate the waves
Tragedy or rhapsody
Nothing in between
The mirror reflects a stranger.

Autumn –
Harvest of life
Roses and thorns
Mountains and valleys
Rejoicing and mourning
The fire burns brightly.
Smoke from fallen leaves
A touch of frost, now and then

Winter –
Twilight
I must light the lamps
Chasing shadows beyond my reach
Ticking of the ancient clock
Embers say it's time to sleep.
No, I'll stir the ashes.
Place a log upon the flame.

One Red Apple

Apple orchard, barren and deserted
Warmed by Indian summer, soon to feel icy fingers of frost
Time for sleep under a mantle of snow
Spicy aroma of apples; fallen, bruised and dying
A few leaves cling tenaciously.
One apple, red and shiny, high on a topmost branch
You shake the tree, I catch the treasure.
We share crisp tartness, remembering perfume of blossoms in May.

I live again the days of country roads at blackberry time.
Birds sing concerts as I search among thorns for the shiny berries.
Nothing compares with warm blackberry pie, enjoyed while rocking on a shady porch.
B.P.

Smoke Dreams

Majestic tree
Sentry of the river
Topmost branches scanning miles of virgin land
Beholding generations come and go
Wigwams, skins stretched taut
Smoke rising toward the sky, then hovering high above the leaves
The scent of corn on heated stones calls hungry children from play.
An old squaw, sewing beads and gazing toward the distant hills
Papoose secure upon her back
Melodies of bird songs for her lullaby
Birch trees, felled and waiting for skillful hands
Canoes that skim streams and navigate rapids deep
Paddles, glistening, flashing in the sun
Trout, iridescent, leaping swiftly over river stones, unknowingly
awaiting spears
Quiver of arrows, hanging from a nearby branch
Hunting yields scanty fare
Ears of corn in golden rows, drying in the sun
Racks of venison, survival until spring appears.
Long, cold winter when snow lies deep
Tree, decades since young braves danced beneath your boughs
Now silence reigns.
When mist rises on the river and the moon is full, do you hear the
tread of moccasins upon the leaves?

Farewell to a Friend

I miss you so.
I whispered goodbye tonight.
Farewell forever

A sentinel, you stood tall and strong.
Leaves softly rustling, a canopy above me
Countless times you were my resting place,
Shelter from burning sun.
I shared secrets as I lay upon the grass,
Alone except for you.
I always knew you would be there.
You laughed and danced amidst the storms as lightening flashed and
thunder rolled.
Battered but not broken
Childhood behind, I left for highways unexplored.
Time passed swiftly, I no longer skipped or ran.
With measured steps I turned toward home.
I recalled the little girl who flew high in a swing,
Reaching out to touch your leaves,
With sorrow, I saw the ravages of time.
You had enemies I never knew.
Slowly they stole your life, almost unnoticed.
You lost the battle.
The crash overwhelmed me.

Cold winds blew tonight.
I placed your final logs upon the fire.
You gave until you had no more to give.
Your ashes I will scatter in the place you called home so many years.
Farewell, dear friend.

Springtime

robins,
   heralds of spring
dragonflies,
   on gossamer wings
violets,
   kissed with dew
misty rainbow,
   bit of heaven

a changeling am I,
   once so sensible
   a realist

now,
   impetuous
   mercurial

walk with me,
   in sunshine,
through raindrops,
   always

Sometimes memory chooses the season we love most.
Springtime, for me, is beginning again.
My world, asleep, under a blanket of snow.
Flowers and tiny blades of grass whisper, "Awaken."
Winter is past.
B.P.

Make Believe World

Beginning at the age of three
Tea parties, empty cups
High heels and mother's hats
A kitty and a dog
No meows and wagging tails
She skipped to school
No teacher, books or friends

At five –
When night came
She lay upon her bed
She talked to Daddy
Though he left three years ago
The toy shoppe, dolls upon the shelf,
"My children," she whispered.

At seven –
Little purse with jingling coins
She could spend them as she pleased
She dreamed of ice cream, cold and sweet
Pocketfuls of candy bars
Cookies with raisins and frosting swirls
Cups of chocolate, afloat with cream

At nine –
In worn-out clothes
Holes in her shoes
She saw herself, shiny slippers, buckles on the top
Warm and wooly coat, fur around her hat
Ribbons and flowers in her hair
Dresses, lace trimmed, rose and blue

At twelve –
She read a fairy tale.
A prince upon a snow white steed
Who rescued maidens in distress.
Riding in the forest green, o'er mountain steep
To the castle with spires high
She wed the prince for happy ever after years.

Elusive hideaway,
Thus she dreamed
One day to wake.
Make-believe was for childhood days.
Sometimes, as she washes windows, cleans the room,
She hears the beat of horse's hooves,
The haunting strains of Lohengrin.

Fairy tales, as a child, became my world.
Memory does not recall when I faced reality.
No lovely gown or handsome prince.
Life has not overwhelmed me.
I have lived in a two room shack, cardboard on the walls.
Decades later, a large, beautiful home.
I have worn old dresses and lovely new gowns.
My treasure I do not hold in my hands.
B.P.

Country Roads

How I miss the old times; days of country roads,
Meandering up hills and into valleys.
Spirals of wood smoke from stone chimneys
Blackberry briers; shiny berries awaiting eager hands.
Homemade signs, "Molasses for Sale."
Country store, where old men gathered
Now, deserted and lonely.

The little wooden church
Women in gingham dresses; men in overalls
Fried chicken, apple pie; dinner on the grounds
Only memories remain.

One room schoolhouse
Boards over windows
No children's voices, waiting for the bell

Someone remembers when the neighbor's barn burned.
Men brought tools, labored by lantern light.

When Joe sat in his chair, weak and pale, they plowed his fields and
planted corn.

The day that Grandma left this world, friends came to mourn.
Singing hymns of long ago
They walked to the grave to say goodbye.

Doors were never locked. How I miss the old times.
Days of country roads

Exchange

When just a child, the days seemed long.
Every day the same
The morning call, "It's breakfast time."
"Come; put your school clothes on."
Out the door
Rain or snow; morning sun with early light
We waited for the summer days
The freedom of barefoot delight
To walk in dew, roaming fields
Chasing fireflies in the night

Oh, to be old enough to choose
What to do and where to go.

Impatiently we wished the years away.
We woke one day to realize the school bell rang for someone else.

Only then we came to know
Freedom is a state of mind.
We exchanged our childhood ways
For rules we did not understand.

As we earn our daily bread,
We say them still, those words we said.
"What to do and where to go."

A Day in Time

Today is mine!
Duty calls; I will not hear.
Today is mine, respite from earthbound.
Breezes like silk kiss my face.
Sunbeams dance before my eyes.
Blossoms share perfume with me.
Concert of birds as butterflies dance
Preview of heaven

Scars

The tree was old and gnarled.
One day branches grew where only scars remain.
I did not see the wounds so long ago.
Life continues; leaves appear again.
With me, as with us all,
Some wounds leave scars that never fade;
Others have been erased with time and love.

Summer Recalled

Summer voices call me
When winter winds blow cold.
The breeze that touched me gently
Becomes a stranger, rough and bold.

The meadow grass, once velvet soft,
Now crackles brown and sear.
It seems like only yesterday
With happy heart I lingered here.

Sunlight, warm and golden,
A carpet of daisies at my feet.
Gossamer wings of butterflies
The scent of clover, honey sweet

Upon the distant hillsides
Stately pines, dark monoliths
Fragrant branches spice the air
Tossed to and fro by shifting winds.

Summer birds have flown away
Leaving doves with mournful sound.
The woodlands silent now
Past glories fallen to the ground

Déjà Vu

Posterity

Walking beside the covered wagon
Oxen drawn,
Piercing eyes, roving endlessly
Wilderness ahead
Faces, leather tanned
The sun like beaten brass
Rain and snow, heat and cold, ~~knowing~~ *gnawing* hunger
Bodies, parched like straw
Coyote howls for lullabies.
Babies left to sleep beneath the sod.
Tears fall in darkness of night.

Look back or turn around –
Never!
What heritage to those I leave behind?
Let them remember I chose the arduous way;
No cheap commitment do I seek.
The price I pay is not too much for me.
My seasoning, a blend of bitter and of sweet
I do not fear to venture where eagles soar.
Wings are strong that beat against the storm.
Let it not be said I did not taste it all.

Hope

From a cocoon, a butterfly,
No longer a prisoner of the past
From ashes of intimate grief
Tomorrow unfolds, no broken promises

Bright shining hours, vivid as a photograph
I delight in remembering the joy of a thousand yesterdays.

Yesterdays

How can it be?
Are these the feet that skipped so lightly down the path?
Are these the hands that plucked the berries from the grass and
carried daisies home?
Are these the arms that held babies as they slept?
Are these the eyes that viewed mountains tall and pictured distant
lands I'd never seen?
In memory, so long ago,
I now recall the ancients as they sat upon their chairs.
With withered hands and misty eyes they reminisced of days gone by.
"It seems like yesterday," they said.
In my youth I asked, "How can it be?"
Now I understand.
Yesterdays now live with me.

A Quiet Place

Amazing!
An old lady at evening time, alone with my memories.
At age 50 did I see myself alone at 90, living again a lifetime?
Never!
They have been patiently waiting.

Friendship

Why did I choose you as my friend?
I've never really known;
A certain something I cannot name.
You did not expect from me what I could not give.
We've climbed mountains and walked through valleys,
Sharing laughter and tears.
When my wounds were more than I could bear,
I knew you would bind them with tender care.
So many miles we've walked the road of life.
Times when we have not agreed, we've built a bridge of love.
Tides of change have swept our shores.
I cannot see the turning in the road ahead.
You may choose another path;
Time may hide your face but suddenly, one day, you will appear.
We shall walk as one again.

Writer's Legacy

Pieces of paper, tiny notes
Tucked away, here and there
Thoughts from flights of fancy
Long forgotten, when or where.

Decision

Where do I go when there is no one?
No one to help lift the burden of failure
In the ashes of defeat I lie.
Despair lurks in the shadows,
Watering the garden of failure with tears.
No blossoms
Reason knocks at the door; I do not answer.

I looked ~~about~~ above the clouds; God smiled.
"Do you not know, my child?
Peace does not dwell with fear and anger.
Close the door on yesterday!
The sun has set.
There are no tears on tomorrow's page."

Fruition

Life.
Sometimes light, sometimes darkness,
Gray, sometimes blue
Radiance of topaz; a few golden hours
Freshness of youth to last rays of sunset,
So many pathways
Phantom footsteps erased at twilight.

Sing no sad songs.
There is a place for you in the sun.

Keeper of Peace
In Memory of Those Who Gave Their Lives

"Goodbye, see you soon!"
In happy years we speak so casually.
Sometimes, never meant to be

Strong arms, invincible, enfolding me
"Goodbye."
First steps of a long journey

A boy who heard the words "be careful" countless times.
My voice, now beyond his recall

Hope erased by dark clouds.
I do not hear the guns or see the fire;
They hover out of reach.
Fear, then despair

Dear friend,
"As you stand with me today midst flowers and tears;
Soft light on the beloved face,
Your hand on mine is not enough.

I need to hear your memories.
Tell me you loved him; the joy he brought you."

Words to remember when nights are dark and long

Let us not speak of what might have been.
Far away years, when our faces are lined with ravages of time and
disappointment,
We will remember him;
Not worn or disillusioned.

In memory
Smiling face, strong arms that held me shall remain forever young.

Labor

Labor bought me silver.
Labor bought me gold.
It paid for land I live on.
It gave me wealth untold.
It paid for food fit for a King when I dined sumptuously.
It didn't pay for sunsets or moonlit nights in spring.
Stars that ride the heavens high
The song of birds that sing
It didn't pay for flower's perfume upon the gentle breeze.
It couldn't buy the ocean waves;
Treasures from the sea.
No gold enough to pay for the love of faithful friends
When they held me in their arms, my broken heart to mend.

Labor brought me weariness at the closing of the day
When the hand of Death comes past to beckon me away.
The only thing I have to keep is what I give away.

Fair Play

A beautiful girl
He sold her a car.
They fell in love and married.
The old car was a piece of junk.
He repaired it and it ran like new.
It's known as negotiation.

Song for a Summer Morning

Stifling heat of yesterday, forgotten.
Stars slowly fade.
Mysterious; stirring in field and forest.
Summer sun filters through curtains of dawn.
Sunbeams reach nests in tree tops,
Bird songs; unwritten symphonies
Minstrels not begging silver
Tiny wrens, raucous jays, feeding,
Demanding young, nearly grown.
Doe and fawn with lustrous eyes depart their leafy refuge.
Stately trees stand not far from where their fathers stood.
Untiring bees carry nectar.
The old owl sleeps, unruffled.
Running swiftly through tall grass, field mouse keeps a wary eye for
predators.
Cricket and katydids in concert
Reflection of clouds on a quiet pond
Amidst lily pads, croaking of frogs
Small squirrels playing tag under mother's watchful eyes
Grasshoppers feast on stalks and leaves.
Spider webs rival designer's beauty.
Dragonflies and butterflies

Those who lay a-bed never marveled at tens of thousands of
dew-drops.
A pauper's diamonds
Millionaire on a summer morning.

Old Age

I cut a slice of bread.
Butter, spoon of honey
A cozy cup of tea
Not much
But then
The hungry years have passed from me.

Evening Friend

Had I met you another time and place when life was springtime,
filled with shining dreams,
I would have sensed the caring in your face.
Someone to hold me through life's devious schemes.
With innocence, I believed that love meant trust.
So young was I that promises were true.
Had I met you in springtime, moonlight, stardust;
With tears, I would have cried,
"Take me with you!"

When last we met the sun was sinking low.
At eventide, it seems I see you still.
Ageless, smiling, waving as you go
I've not forgotten you, I never will.

Shadows near, I have a place to hide;
To mourn alone the broken dreams that died.

Heritage

Ancient horse, bones protruding
Old man with gnarled hands
Fingers clutching the rusty plow
Stumbling on freshly turned sod
Footsteps where his father walked
Decades past

Confidence

My teacher stood before the class.
"Next week we have a spelling bee."
Sixth grade students from every school
How exciting! That meant me.

Running home, out of breath,
I couldn't wait to share.
"I wish that I could win;
I have no dress to wear."

"I know that you can do it.
We'll find something," Mama said.
I hoped for something special,
Bright, with flowers pink and red.

Out of a box, an old blue dress,
Not a pretty sight.
"I'll make it over," Mama said.
She cut and sewed that night.

When she put it on me
With a pretty collar made of lace,
Love made the transformation.
I saw the look upon her face.

Up the steps, into the light
I stood at last with trembling heart.
I saw my family watching me,
Impatient for the time to start.

I won the third place ribbon.
Mama said she knew I would.
I knew why I won it,
Because she said I could.

My Shelter

So far removed from yesteryears
Memory eludes me.
Some things I don't recall.
Voices, now silent
Blossoms on a summer day
Their fragrance long forgotten
Never, never land
Unreality

Forgotten are shining hours.
Storms rage.
In the midst of the tempest, my God holds me.

Security

Some live in tents on shifting sand.
Pioneers in cabins of sod,
Log cabins with warm fireplace
Igloos where Eskimos dwell
The poor in a humble cottage
Mansion on the boulevard
Castle with turrets into the sky

What matters, if love dwells within?

Counting the Cost

You wish to view the world from the top?

Treacherous, the quicksand of success
No place for your feet to hesitate
It borders a wide and dangerous sea.
Swift currents carve channels in unexpected places.
Shipwrecks, carnage of centuries, lie at the bottom.

Observe clearly those who have been there.
When you have considered and your dreams have not dimmed,
Enquire of those on the highest pinnacle.
Does gold replace children's goodnight kisses or a loving "Welcome
Home?"
Are they bowed beneath the burden of what might have been?

Hold firmly to the hands of those you love.
Careless hands exchange beauty for ashes.
Success, the intractable taskmaster

Is there a living person who has not
regretted a decision? I think not.
Learning is a part of living.
Pick up the pieces and try again.
B.P.

Nameless

He lay along the road
Beaten, wounded, half dead.
Thieves stole his clothes.
Helpless, naked and alone.
A traveler, well dressed, glanced in his direction;
Crossed to the other side.
Why get involved with a nobody?
Again, the sound of footsteps
A glimpse of fine garments,
Pain-filled eyes watch him pass by.
Is there no one?
A shadow; caring hands reach out.
What does it matter who he is?
Compassion is giving.
It does not turn away.
Binding wounds soils garments but cleanses the soul.

Yesterday?
In your city?
"No."
The road to Jericho
Two thousand years ago
The stranger remains unknown except for the words,
"A certain Samaritan."

Could it be that I may walk that way some day?
It matters not that I remain nameless.
Luke 10:33

Gift of Time

I softly knocked upon the door,
Flowers in my hand.
Touch of brightness in the long, dark hall
The door, paint worn; fingerprints from countless hands
I heard the feeble voice that bid me enter the small, white room.
A worn quilt on a rocking chair
Smiling children in an oval frame
Essence of home
A lifetime knitted and unraveled.
Lovingly, I kissed the wrinkled cheek; gentle smile, sweetened with
time.
Her aged hands spoke volumes.
The chasm between youth and age became only a step.

Days that were no more
Tasting memories that stood firm against waves of loneliness.
She lived again the springtime of life.
Collage of faces, drifting silently, nearly beyond recall
Letting go of yesterdays, she whispered,
"I don't get lonely; I'm happy here."
Winter came to fill her eyes, reality her heart.

Leaving my gift, I tiptoed to the door.
I wish I could believe the words she spoke.
The here and now faded into yesterday once more.

Malaise

Nothing made to cure the ills I feel;
Symptoms I cannot describe.
Hopeless shuffling of countless feet
Wine, making reality a misty haze
Fear that bars windows;
Eyes peering carefully lest enemies approach.
So few the smiles on faces passing by.
How can I live as though the world is singing?

When did the love songs turn to hate?
Why do we look the other way when others cry?
We extend our hands but not too far.
Safer to give silver than dry other's tears
The ultimate is giving strength to one another.
Out of the darkest night and jungle of fear
The sun rises every day.

Every person has been disappointed
sometime in their life.
Take them a flower and a smile.
B.P.

A Daughter to her Father

It is too late.
You lie beneath the sod, the woods you loved surrounding you.
How well I remember the trees – walnut, oak, maple –
Your saw and plane transforming them to works of art.
I learned so young; my childish voice did not question.
You did not wish to hear.
I never felt your arms around me.
Your carpenter's hands stroked wood, which had no life, but never
smoothed my hair.
I never heard the words, "I love you."
Perhaps you spoke them secretly as I lay in my little bed.
Sounds without meaning
I will never know.
Words you measured out to me, so few,
spelled only failure, never praise.
My teenage longing, hidden from your eyes
Your chair was empty on my graduation day.
I did not exist for you, except another mouth to feed.

A woman grown, I tried to please.
With time I understood, you had never loved.
Forgiving you released me to love you.
I don't know why you grew sharp thorns instead of flowers.
They wounded me so many times.
I cleansed the wounds with love and tried again.

Working beside you in the soil, your hands so
carefully nurturing growing things.

You, who were once so strong, now leaned upon my arm.
Miles we traveled with my hands upon the wheel.
When did you know I was worthy of your trust?
Did you realize your mortality when you looked at me?
No longer a child beside you, time had stolen our days.

How sad that old age slowed your steps but scarcely
warmed your heart.
If you could sit with me today, would you smile
at me and hold my hand?
I will never know.
There is forever silence where you sleep.

Because of you, wherever I have lived, I've planted flowers.

The Empty Place

"It is not time," He said.

Living in the midst of chaos;
Hate and darkness surround me.
I long to hear the trumpet sound.

"It is not time," He said.

You told me there awaits me
Purest gold and jewels rare.
No disappointment or broken dreams.

"It is not time," He said.

My eyes, blinded with tears.
I know not where to go.
This is not my home.

"It is not time," He said.

"Dry your tears that you may see;
The work is not finished.
Behold, the fields are ripe unto harvest."

"It is not time," He said.
St. John 4:35

Mélange of Daydreams

Narrow country road, the day newly born.
Created for a vagabond
Glittering dewdrops, sunbeams filtering through emerald leaves
Suddenly, a tiny lane; grass covered.
Old gate; beckoning me, as if to say, "Come in"
Each step takes me back to an era, far removed.
An old chimney, built of field stones, a few charred timbers,
All that remains of someone's dreams.
Weathered barn, silver gray, looking frail, bones holding it together
are tired.
Rough-hewn logs, notched by careful hands.
Perhaps, one day it sheltered cattle, a horse or two.
The sound of milk, warm and foaming, playing a tune as it strikes
the pail.
The scent of clover mingled with country air.
Gnarled apple tree, cloud of pale and fragrant blooms,
Once a year restored to youth
Clothed in a gown to cover branches, aged and scarred,
Enticing bees, sharing nectar
May Day celebration

From ashes of the past it seems I see a slender
lass with long, brown hair.
Sunbonnet of gingham to shade rosy cheeks
Lingering glances at the precious baby, asleep beneath the lilac bush.
Wrapped in blankets sewn with love by candle light
Strong brown hands pulling weeds, impatient for harvest
In the cabin, soup bubbles merrily upon the old wood range.
Brown, crusty bread baked in Grandma's heavy pans

Golden butter churned from rich cream
Supper for a hungry man, weary from plowing
fields and cutting wood

Evening shadows bring night creature sounds.
Time for sharing dreams
Slowly, I return to find a silent world.
Where have they gone?

Far away, somewhere, an old man in a rocking chair,
Living again his childhood days
Helping with evening chores
How sweet the apples, come September
Winter night
Firelight dancing, warm and bright

In memory, time stands still.
Down the lane, home remains evergreen.

My Heritage

Out of the darkness – Light!
The Supreme Architect
God of Creation, brought forth –
Rolling seas
Majestic mountains
Melody of streams
God said, "It is good."

Grass
Flowers, waving in gentle breezes
Trees, laden with fruit

The command, "Let there be --."
Sunbeams
Moonbeams
Shining stars

Creatures, great and small
On land and sea

Silence of space
Vast expanse
Solitude

You are after His likeness
Have you walked alone?
How does one define loneliness?

Creatures without understanding

Fragrance of flowers
Concert of birds

Precious jewels
Gold and silver

The God of Creation desiring something more
Someone to say, "I love you."

Adam –
You are His masterpiece
Fashioned with care
Surrounded with perfection

Sharing your life –

Eve –
Stirring Satan's envy

Satan –
Presenting what he did not possess

Jesus –
Born to die that I may live

He is not a stranger to me.
His words have become mine.
Another time and place I shall see Him.

Left behind; a few tattered threads

Reflection

I envy not the wealthy their possessions.
I shall never know the price they paid.
It was not always so.
There was a day I gazed in awe.
I could not fathom a life of wealth, surrounded with my heart's
desires.
Richness of velvet
Candle glow
Silver gleaming
A dream to me; the rich consider commonplace
Someday, I too, shall dine gourmet.

The young, seated across my table tonight,
See themselves where I now sit.
Richness of velvet
Candle glow
Silver gleaming
Stars in their eyes speak the word,
"Someday."
I look at them and remember.
Those who live for someday may cross barren deserts.
A candle glows in a cottage or a mansion.
Share your bread with delight.
Happiness is love reflected.

Abbey - Kilarney, Ireland

Stones, grimy with soot of decades,
Smoke from coal and turf blown by capricious winds
No living to remember masons, high on scaffolds,
laying weighty stones,
with pride placing the final stone
Spire reaching toward heaven
Family tales, passed from generations past
Oak benches, scarred from the faithful, rich and
poor kneeling in reverence,
sometimes drying a tear
Aged women, with snowy hair, softly repeating responses
remembered from childhood
Worn prayer books in gnarled hands, petitions like old friends
Aged priest, dozing fitfully, nodding, perhaps recalling service in a
far-away land among strangers; longing for the green Irish hills to live
sunset years among his own.
Who remembers gifted hands that fashioned angels
and the Christ child?
Somewhere, on moldy, mildewed pages they live on.
The young priest, with lively steps, enters to light the candle,
Soft light shining upon the words of Jeremiah, "the weeping prophet,"
his words living once more.
Bright flowers, warm serene surroundings,
perhaps in memory of a loved one
I silently walk upon stones trod by multitudes,
moments etched between the past and the present.
Quiet respite from a chaotic world

The Seeker

Where have they gone?
Men without guile
Honorable men
Unashamed to meet enquiring eyes
Are we so far removed from landmarks
written in stone by the hand of God?
Justice, standing afar off
Judgment, turned away backward
Truth, fallen in the streets,
trampled by careless feet
Slowly dying, almost unnoticed
Someday, perhaps, someone will ask,
"Is this where truth once lived?"
No one will remember
Isaiah 59:14

We have within us a compass God gave us for direction.
I had a dish of chocolates on a coffee table when my
great-grandson came to visit. He was about 1 ½ years of age.
We were in another room and did not notice when he
left the room. We located him behind a chair with his mouth
filled with chocolate. No one had told him not to touch
the chocolates. Why did he hide?
Adam and Eve are an example. The seeds we plant are
the ones that grow.
May our gardens flourish with truth.
B.P.

The Journey

In a world of discontent, midst wealth and poverty;
Angels sang.

Why did angels sing?
Celebration of hope!

Mary, mother of Jesus, chosen to love this child; both mother and
servant

At twelve, His calling has come;
Separation to prepare to sacrifice himself
Years of preparation, a glimpse of the future
No crown or royal robes; a King with dusty feet
Time for His chosen ones –
Doctor, fishermen, tax collector
Eleven faithful; one a deceiver, betrayer for gold
Baptism; a few years before teaching
Days of fasting and prayer
Words recorded that we might follow.

Day of departure
Sentence of death, reason He was born
The cup of suffering, His to drink

"King of the Jews"
His enemies spoke the truth.

Broken-hearted mother as blood flowed from the cross
Hammer echoes; thrust of the sword

Darkness descends
It is finished.

Death is swallowed in victory.

Let us not forget.
The journey is nearly finished.

The hopeless weep.
The redeemed rejoice.

Remembrances

Between the pages of a book
Blossoms, faded and forgotten
Wild clover
Fragrance beyond recall

Nearly erased with time,
I remember –

Shimmering summer sunlight
Sparkling diamonds of morning dew
Carefree roaming in shades of emerald –
Through fragile mist I remember you.

Winds of change have blown away
That long ago enchanted day.

Royalty

Majestic eagle
King of heights
Wild and free
Noble, unafraid

Long, broad wings
Soaring with currents

Powerful sweep
Lightning speed

Bird of prey
Plunging swiftly, silently
Hunger driven

Courting time
Cartwheels and spirals
Mating for life

Tallest trees, rocky cliffs
Castle in the sky

May the day never come
When man, his only enemy
Brings this
Prince of Splendor
To mortality

We identify birds by their distinctive
songs and habits. God could have
made replicas of one bird
with one song.
There is no one like you.
God loves variety.

B.P.

Summer Rain

Turmoil of clouds
Gray tinted sky
Capricious gusts of wind
Phantom mist drifts by

Suddenly, the sun!

Raindrops like crystal beads
Azure sky through gray
Fleecy clouds on high
Breezes sweeping mist away

Rainbow's joyous message
Heaven's gift, a summer day

I close my eyes and once again
remember summer rain.
Dark clouds, opening with their gift
of warm raindrops, running
like rivers on my face.
A mermaid child.
B.P.

Gypsy

Windows need washing
The house isn't neat.
There's dust on the table
And nothing to eat.

I should write a letter.
Someone may call.
It's not that I'm lazy,
Just tired of it all.

I'd love to go roaming
As I did long ago.
Walk by the river
Where cypress trees grow

Holes in my shoes
My dress is all faded.
I know what to do
When life becomes jaded.

I'll run with the wind
Laugh at the rain
Until not a vestige
Of troubles remain.

I'll revel in freedom
Bask in the sun –
A place filled with magic
Where daydreams are spun.

The day's nearing sunset –
Departing too soon
The life of a gypsy
For one afternoon

City of Light

Paris
No longer the sound of war
Scars have disappeared, disguised by clever hands
Mannequins stare sightlessly through elegant shop windows
Close of day, sunset on the river Seine
Lovers strolling in a world apart
Glimmering lights reflecting on the boulevard
Tiny sparrows flutter among the leaves, blending their evening songs
with haunting strains of violins
Love themes drifting from a small café
Music of quiet laughter
Shadows conceal a table for two
Candle light; ardent glances
Engraved forever in memory
A miser of happy moments
I live again
Enchanting violins
Candle glow
Magic of a summer night
The ecstasy of Paris

Some memories never fade.
Paris, I've never forgotten you.
B.P.

Anticipation

God knew me before I saw the light of day.
A child, my thirst for knowledge overwhelmed me.
Living countless lifetimes on a carpet of dreams
Printed pages, gift of strangers
Standing upon a castle wall, my faded dress became a silken gown
Breezes from unseen mountains caressed me
A dreamer
Poverty decrees I dwell in an ancient house,
icy winds against my window panes.

Someday

Years disappear into eternity –
Thirst for knowledge; unabated

How to understand?
I knew not.

The light of God shining in my mind ever-seeking

Years of joy and sorrow
Precious children –
One I hold in my arms,
One to God for safe keeping

Always – the Shadow of God's presence

Decades –
Where have they gone?
Chained to tempted flesh, God securely holds me.
With love He comforts me, patiently prepares me for this moment;
a door I have never opened –

Day's End

I am not ready for the sun to set.
Weeds to pull, seeds to plant
Dusk has settled in the hollows.
The range of hills reflects the fading light of day.
Dew, fallen cool upon the grass

Reluctantly my footsteps turn toward home.
Familiar path so many years
I'll find it though my eyes grow dim.
Isolation of darkness
I walk along
Wrapped in my cloak of Aprils past.

There were eight children in our family.
My mother was ordered by my father to supervise our work
in the garden as he worked away from home during the week.
We depended on vegetables for food. We walked between rows
with cans of kerosene and sticks and knocked worms and bugs
into the kerosene. When my father came home, we followed behind
as he walked between rows. He said nothing, just pointed at the worms
and bugs we missed. How I hated gardening!
Can you believe that 50 years later I planted a garden?
B.P.

Ethereal

let this be love,
not just a passing moment.
dreams are fragile
like mist in the early ~~mourn~~ *morn*.
music, laughter, endearment
then
suddenly gone.
let this be love,
not a brief time of
fascination.
elusive as moonbeams
restless
as waves of the sea
longing for trust and comfort
with
honest emotion
could it be
love passed by unknowingly?
let this be love
sharing of heartbreak and pleasure
ethereal beauty
or
treacherous fury of storm
a dreamer
who reaches for happiness
beyond measure
weaving a cloak of fantasy
idyllic and warm
softly
enchanting music
and laughter
let this be love
this moment and ever after

Interlude

Summer days
of endless heat
torrid waves
from city streets

A bright green bench
inviting me
sheltered by
a gnarled, old tree

Perfect place
for lemonade

Time
for daydreams
in the shade

Tiny flowers
scattered
in the grass

Ice
making music
in my glass

The melody
a dreamer's song

Tranquility
midst
a restless throng

Journey on a Mountain Road

Off the beaten track, a winding road;
far from the rush of shiny metal
on cement ribbons
Weathered cabin, slanted with time
Rough hewn logs, split wood shingles
Porch braided rugs and rocking chairs
Battered screen door; scarred by impatient paws of hounds
Red bud tree casts a glow of spring time magic
Well-tended garden, promise of summer harvest
Clothes, drying on the fence

Tiny mountain woman, shaded by sunbonnet
Back bent; long years of labor, dawn till dusk
Toting water from the spring, scrubbing on the wash board
Birthing babies; teaching them old country ways
Contentment with a gentle smile

Ancient hillsman, bronze from the sun
His faded shirt and old plow shoes speak of
communion with the earth

To and fro they rock in silence
Companions for a lifetime

The rutted road continues past briar thickets

Silver gray mill hanging o'er the stream
Millwheel slowly turning
Inside, the dust of decades from grinding grain clings to

rafters, secured by cobwebs
Early morn, old men shoulder bags of wheat and corn
Millstones grinding grain to flour and meal

Outside the mill
Chickens, unhampered by wire and posts, scratch
for grain,
if by chance kernels fall from bags

Brown-eyed Susans decorate the wayside
In the meadow a brindle cow grazes placidly
Farmer with strong, sinewy arms, bound to the mule and plow
with long straps of worn leather
Turning furrows of sandy loam, damp and rich
Apple orchard, trees attired in showy gowns
In autumn
Hanging iron kettles
Flames dancing as women stir
Scent of apple butter, spicy and dark

Mountain man; gnarled fingers plucking strings of a battered banjo
Old feet tapping time to familiar melodies

Generations past who faced life with dignity
Accepting hardship as a way of life

The young have gone
Cabins and cornbread don't satisfy their appetites
They have left the old country church for cathedrals on city streets

Baying of hounds, cawing of crows; lonesome sounds

Logs decay
Chimneys crumble
The mill stands silent
From meadows, hills and orchards
One by one
Sojourners on their journey to the Promised Land

In a quiet corner, moss covered gravestones

If you are weary of this busy, confused world,
find a quiet place and live a day through
the eyes of yesterday.
B.P.

Midnight

Candles of star shine
Black velvet skies
Melodious music
Night wind sighs
Silver moonbeams
Caressing my face
Celestial moments
Time can't erase

Good Fortune

Eagerly I searched for beauty.
I found it in a maid so fair.
She was a dream come true.
Entranced, I lingered there.

She held a mirror to her face.
Never looked away
I spoke to her so soft and sweet.
She didn't have a word to say.

I wandered down a country lane.
A maiden I met along the way.
She bid me sit and rest awhile.
I eat bread with honey every day.

Secrets

Country homestead
Deserted
Windows like empty eyes
Fallow fields
The only sound, tiny feet of mice that scurry on the dusty attic floor
Tucked under rafters, concealed from curious hands
Journal of parchment, faded and stained, penned with passion from a
solitary heart
Endearing phrases; not meant for stranger's eyes
The writer, long at rest beneath a marble stone
Thoughts, uninvited, bid me share my secret world.

Forbidden fruit
I shall never write the words.
They have blown away –
Whispers in the wind.

We purchased an old farm, a century old,
original family. No one had changed it.
In the attic I found an old diary.
B.P.

Tapestry

Twilight time
Peaceful interlude
Thoughts – nomads drifting
Smiles and tears, kinship with moments past
Clock on the mantel
The hands no longer moved
Time had gone, I knew it not
Wandering back in memory, when days seemed infinite, filled with
promise
I longed for loved ones to remain forever young
I wished to stop the world; the beauty of it all
With pensive heart I closed that door.

I remembered other days when life was filled with pain and fear.
Tears coursed like rivers down my face.
I wished that I could change my heartache into joy.
Erase the pain

Time became my friend and gently dried my tears.
Tangled skeins of life became a tapestry,
Some bright, some dark.

I'll never see the finished work.
Someone will say,
"The bouquet is faded now."
For a passing moment
An illusion of radiance remains.

Climb With Me

I have walked the low road –
Pathway of privation.
Who remembers childhood poverty?
Those cast in a different mold
Long years past; not forgotten
Memory living yesteryears again

One lovely day the clouds lifted.
I glimpsed a road far above, glistening in the sun.
I was not created for lowlands.
Scars I bear remind me of battles, fought and won.
Hillsides of rocks did not turn me aside.
Bruises and tears; my companions
The last mile
Triumphantly, my final step
Beckoning to others far below.

Are you walking through an arid land
this moment? Springtime grass has withered.
Flowers without courage to blossom.
You are not alone.
God knows when a sparrow falls to earth.
Matthew 10:29

B.P.

Never to be Forgotten
1927 - 1937

September and new shoes
First day of school
Choosing one piece of penny candy
Collecting warm eggs from under the hen
Learning to roller skate
Trading sandwiches with school friends
Playing jacks on the porch steps
Flying kites in the March wind
Chasing fireflies after sunset
Holding the lantern as Mom milks the cow
Sitting near the stove on a cold winter's night
Wind whistling in the chimney
Potatoes baking in the cookstove oven
Telling scary stories in the dark
Sleeping on the sheets dried in the sun
Pancakes for breakfast; Saturday morning
Eating tomatoes, warmed by the sun
Tapping for luck when you see the first robin
Swinging in the tire swing
Building a tree house
Sharing secrets with your best friend
Report card day
Riding a friend's pony
Homemade bread, hot from the oven
Wild blackberries along the roadside
Looking for a rainbow after a shower
Searching for four leaf clovers
Fireworks on the Fourth of July
New family in the neighborhood
First date
Goodbye to childhood

Indian Summer

Time has flown since leaves appeared.
Courtship of birds, flirtatious and bold
Warm and moist, the earth nurtured seeds
Bountiful harvest now past
Dry stalks of corn
A few tomatoes on the vines
Marigolds glow like captive sunbeams.
Summer sun wears an autumn face.
Chill winds send ~~swallow~~ swallows south.
The last crisp apples
Aflame; leaves scatter.
Nimble squirrels hoard fallen nuts.
Summer's last curtain call, reluctant to say goodbye
Farewell finale; Indian summer

Something melancholy about the
last days of summer. Walking through
a vineyard, a few bunches of grapes remain;
revealed now that grape leaves
have withered with frost.
Another harvest past.
B.P.

True Love

Her lovely smile won me over. *forever.*
I pray that we shall never part.
She didn't care that I was poor.
No mansion or diamonds to win her heart

My darling was only three months old.

Why?

Dark and ominous clouds
Charcoal sky
Why is the mocking bird singing?
The song continues.
Suddenly
Capricious spring

Memories

The chair was ancient; springs broken,
Cover, faded and tattered.
Daddy's chair until he left
Afterward, Mama sat there.
The old house sold.
"I'll take the chair," she said.
"A new one?"
"Oh, no!"
It must have been the dreams nestled there.

Spin Doctors

They taught him how to walk and talk
Subjects not to speak about
When to say "yes" and when to say "no"
They created a hero, there is no doubt
Most times life reaps just what you sow
Crowds saw the emperor wore no clothes

Election Year

The air is filled with verbalism.
Candidates with egotism
The public hears with cynicism.
Diagnosis – moral aneurysm

Who

It was a lovely little town
Officials served with pride
Problems solved with scarcely a frown
No one cheated or lied

When last month's bills came due
The money had disappeared
Suspicious eyes asked, "Who?"
Some mistrusted, others feared

Officials stood before the judge
One by one they said, "Not me."
After investigation
They found "Not me" had done it

Sands of Time

Some live for tomorrow
When life will be perfect
So they dream
The sun rises and sets
Flowers blossom and die
Some seek fortune tellers
Searching for futures that never shall be
Waiting for someone to listen
Sand in the hourglass of time
How quickly the grains fall!
Today is precious

To a Friend

Come, stand beside me in the sun
How pale your face and cold your hand
Living in shadows, your world has faded
After grief there is time to heal
A time to keep and a time to cast away
Keep the sweetness
Cast away the bitter

Look toward the distant hills!
A rainbow over the valley
Rainbows appear when storms are past

Come, stand beside me in the sun

Renewal

'Tis spring
and
once again
tiny buds
peep from
weathered stalks
forces of
life
flow strong
where
no one sees.
years
of sun and storms
have
passed me by
leaving
lines and shadows.
I ask
that every springtime
of my life
my
leaves
grow strong
until
the lines
and shadows disappear
and
only leaves
remain

Contemplations of Job

Job spoke, "Let the day perish wherein I was born.
The Almighty troubleth me.
He thundereth marvelously with His voice.
He directeth His lightning unto the ends of the earth.
We cannot comprehend.
Hath the rain a father?
Who hath begotten the dew?
The balancing of clouds
Small rain and great rain
Can we lift our voice that abundance of water covers us?
He quieteth the earth with the south wind."

Out of the whirlwind God questions,
"Who is this that darkens counsel by words without knowledge?
Hast thou given peacocks their beauty or wings and
feathers unto the ostrich?
Does the hawk fly by thy wisdom and the eagle
mount at thy command?
Who hath given wisdom and understanding to the heart?
Where were you when I laid the foundations of the earth?
Who laid the measure and stretched the line?
Where were you when the morning stars sang together?
Who shut up the sea and stayed the proud waves?
Thus far shalt thou come and no further.
Hast thou walked in search of the depth of the sea?
Who gendered the hoary frost of heaven?
Hast thou entered into the treasures of snow and hail?
How is light parted from darkness?

Hast thou commanded the morning since thou wast born?
Where is the place where light and darkness dwell?
Hast thou lived so long thou knoweth the path
to the house where they live?
Wilt thou disannul my judgment?
Have the gates of death been opened unto thee?

Job answered the Lord, "I have uttered that which I understood not."

Fountain of Youth

Thirst for youth is born when youth has disappeared.
The fountain flowed unheeded as seasons passed.
Quest for excitement erased the search for life's meaning.
Tasting the moment; taking, giving nothing in return
The fountain scarcely flows
Enough to enjoy with the residue of life.

Comfort

A closeness born of sorrow
The cup from which you drink once was mine.
I reach out to you.
No words or celestial music
No balm for despair
Simply a touch of love

Quiet Time

House filled with children
Laughter and tears
A meadow; my quiet place
No sound except a cricket's song

Visions became reality.
My diary; joy and sorrow
City streets and country roads
Sunrise and sunset

Voices, forever silent

Decades past, miles behind
My chair; my quiet place
Somewhere a cricket sings, and the sun is shining.

Nearly every person who has lived many decades
reminisces of the past. As a child,
waiting for a special day seemed forever.
Cherish each day as we shall not pass this way again.
B.P.

Reaching for Maturity

"Someday you'll understand, when you are older."
The answer came, again and again.
Someday has come and gone.
Questions I asked then I don't ask now.
The answers are not important.
Questions I ask now have no answers, or those I ask don't know.
I've ridden the crest of waves that filled my eyes with hopeless tears.
Battered, life thrust me upon the rocky shore.
Bruises heal, tears disappear.
Tell me –
Does maturity come with time or endurance?

There are people, who make unwise decisions,
living with regret a lifetime.
If we refuse to learn from life,
we will continue our journey,
filled with sorrow and remorse.
Only One who walked on earth was perfect.
B.P.

Ghost Town

Death of a village
Weathered sign, hanging by a nail or two
"Gas and Groceries"
Broken, weathered and gray
Leaning like tired, old men
Children's feet once danced on sagging floors
Doors askew
Broken window panes
Tattered curtains flutter in the wind.
Last remnant of home
Sunset's afterglow softens harsh angles
Deserted and silent
Darkness is kind to the village someone called home.

What a contrast between our
brightly lighted cities with marble buildings,
skyscrapers, restaurants and parks!
Planes, taxicabs and limousines.
Luxuries become commonplace.
Far back in time there were people
willing to sacrifice;
a debt which we can never repay.
B.P.

Shamrocks and Rainbows

Galway, Kilarney, County Kerry
Names that bring tears to those who left the old sod, never to return
Driven by famine, thousands sailed to strange lands.
Never an Irishman who has no story to tell; the magic
of the Blarney Stone
Emerald Isle, where life is gentle and time stands still.
Stark cliffs, swept by sea foam
Meadows and fields
Sheep grazing near a small stream, wending its way to the sea
Wisps of smoke rising from the chimney of a thatched roof
Cottage walls darkened from decades of peat fires
Fences of weathered stone, worn smooth through eons of time
Meadows of haystacks
Farmers, with pitchforks, tossing hay onto a wagon; piled high, the
horse pulls the wagon homeward.
A narrow track, the road to the village, rutted and rough
The old blacksmith, with calloused hands, at the forge, a horse
patiently waiting
Neighbors at the village pub, delaying failure and
debt with words and laughter
Those who yearn for sights beyond the village and mountains follow
the road past timeless castle ruins, once home of earls and lords
Remains of past grandeur, now silent
On streets, over ancient bridges, the river flows through arches as it
has for centuries
From humble abodes to costly mansions, soft light filters through
windows hung with elegant Irish lace
Shopkeepers, with smiling eyes, pass the time of day
with soft lilting cadence
Shops, once owned by ancestors who now rest in
the nearby church yard
Gravestones covered with moss

Abbey; stone floor, trod by those who withdrew from
the world for a lifetime of prayer
Magnificent cathedral
Worshippers kneeling where Irish have knelt for centuries

Crystal, crafted by men with pride and love of beauty, passed from
generation to generation

Beyond city streets, gently mountains and vales beckon
Melody of waterfalls and bird songs
Casting in the stream rippling over rocks, the fisherman waits
patiently for wary trout

Kissed by sun, rain and mist, living forever in the hearts of those
whose feet have trod the land of shamrocks and rainbows

Sea Dreamer
Veendam 2005

Who was the first dreamer with a vision of a palace on the high seas?

Opulence greater than ancient kings possessed

Tropic sun's rays forbidden to disturb the comfort of the privileged;
somewhere far below, unseen hands control tropic air

I close my eyes and imagine a cool, shady forest.

Soft light upon linen cloths
China, crystal, silver

Afternoon tea, gracious interlude
Memory of a far distant past

Muted tones; piano and violin recall Vienna

Quiet corner; a book if desired

Thirst for excitement?
Bars
Casinos
Theater
Youth meet to dance
The aged to remember

Men, once young, shrunken with age, scuffle slowly, viewing art
treasures through jaded eyes, days long past to conquer the world
Youth has fled, exchanging time for fool's gold,
leaving only riches and luxury

Far removed, on poverty-stricken islands,
young men reluctantly leave home.

Their destination; a great ship, filled with people searching
for escape from an everyday world

Arms that harvested fish now carry trays.

Their home, a small bed and food in the depth of the ship

Escaping poverty, they have become prisoners of their choosing.

Smiling and gracious, we do not see the homesick hearts or
tears shed silently in lonely darkness of night.

As the great ship slowly moves from the harbor, the sun bids us
farewell as it slowly disappears into the sea; its final rays caress the
waves.

Moon and stars appear on the velvet curtain of night.

Another day until reality calls us to our familiar world.

Bon Voyage!

Interlude at Sea
2005

The great ship glides quietly toward tropical shores, soft light and
music to erase life's realities

How can it be that I, a child of poverty, gaze upon a calm sea, as the
sun disappears on its long journey to the far side of the world?

Beneath waves, wondrous mysteries

In long past childish dreams, I would someday feast on my heart's
desires; someone to grant the least of my wishes

What words to express my gratitude that God should grant me
luxuries when there are those surviving on a crust of bread?

Let me not forget, when this day becomes another of life's memories,
may the peace of this moment survive through stormy days.

Times when I cannot understand the demands life had thrust upon
me and my heart is weary and I long for the perfection of Heaven

Sanctuary

Long shadows shroud the sundial's face.
Time to forsake the familiar
Currents of change sweep near me, unseen.
My roots grow in shallow places.
They flourish wherever I am planted.
I have escaped the insidious pull of mire.
My days; seasoned with spice
Waterfalls in mountains, streams in valleys
Music of the earth is ever near.
Symphonies of endless melodies
Some melancholy, some jubilant
Fireflies and chandeliers illumine my life.
I am not enclosed by walls.
Peaceful is my heart.
The sun is not limited to one horizon.

Afterglow

Bright shining hours
Vivid, as a photograph
I delight in remembering
the joys of a thousand
yesterdays

Paper Mâche Crowns
Jerry Garcia
"The Grateful Dead"

He died.
The faithful wept a million tears.
Drugs were comfort until they became his master.
Silent cries for help, haunted with fears
Life in the fast lane raced a little faster.
No one reigns supreme in this kingdom for long.
Some crowns are paper mâche, not pure gold
A bright, new star is born for the price of a song.
Fickle the mistress success; unfaithful and cold
Fragile; crushed and broken, unable to fly
Crowds disappear, no longer the sound of mirth
Who remains to dry tears when the lonely cry?

Laid aside the mask of 'let's pretend'
No one near to hear the last note end

Jerry Garcia was a victim of drugs.
He made the decision to enter
drug treatment. When he did not appear
someone entered his room. He died alone.
B.P.

Rebirth

Light of day begins to fade
Shadows of night my world invade
Shut out darkness, pull the shade
Time to reflect

Words that cause my heart to break
Searching for a road to take
Life's misfortunes to forsake
Nowhere to run

What of impossible battles won?
What of lovely days in the sun?
What of dreams so often spun?
Is all in vain?

Sunrise as I stroll the shore
Footprints where I walked before
New day; my spirit to restore
Rebirth at dawn

Dawning

Night lingers
Dawn hides in a shroud of mist
Hushed stillness as stars pale
First notes of a robin
Explosion of joy –
The sun rises

Runaway

Who has not wished to run away?
A child of six, not certain you belong
Heaviness in your heart
Winters early twilight steals away the sun
The wind, sharp and cold
Fingers, tingling with frost

Alone
Huddled in your tiny hiding place

Mother's voice
Faintly calling, "Come home."

So many unknowns in darkness
You remember there is a place for you

Warm glow as you open the door
Familiar voices

Aroma of freshly-baked bread
Your chair at the table

No longer Mother calls your name
Home lies in memory
No longer a child, although sometimes
Who does not wish to run away?

Continuity

So lovingly, I cared for it and watched it grow.
One glorious morn it burst in showers of fragrant bloom.
A bit of heaven here on earth!
How sad to see it quickly fade
Blossoms for a day

It is now time to plant a tree.
One day it will stand tall and strong.
Its boughs may shield a traveler from the sun,
Shade to cool his brow.
He will never know once flowers blossomed here.
It seems the perfume is with me still.

Some things are meant to last but for a day.
Memory keeps them ever near.

*The company where I worked had
changed landscaping. They previously had hundreds
of hybrid iris. They placed them where we could
choose some for our homes. Magnificent flowers
in many colors. I left that house many years ago.
Each springtime, I am happy knowing they
bring happiness to someone I will never know.*
B.P.

Dreams

I must put them all away
Mementoes from another day
Eons ago
Unbidden, they appear
Unexpected times
Perfume in the air
Gentle breeze, sighing in the trees
Mocking bird singing in the night
Moonlit shadows through the leaves
Images, sometime so near
I swiftly turn to see the face that isn't there
Reluctantly, I wake to face reality

Contemplation

Do you ever ask, what might have been?
I remember a summer day –
Children with their mother.
She was the treasure of our lives.
"What if you'd married someone else?"
"Who would we have been?"
She didn't smile.
Years later, I understood.

Crossroads

I held the map, crisscrossed with lines, confused as to direction.
Someone afar off running swiftly
His eyes danced as he came near.
"Come with me.
"My name is Excitement."
I smiled and said, "Perhaps someday."
He waved and quickly disappeared.
A carriage amidst a cloud of dust
One sharp command, the coachman stopped
Regal man in elegant garments
"Come with me.
"My name is Wealth."
I smiled and said, "Perhaps someday."
Imperiously, the carriage rolled away.
Decision time, the day far spent
The sound of singing
Serenade of a happy soul
Over the hill, a wayfarer
Worn shoes, mended cloak
With radiant face, he spoke.
"Come with me.
"My name is Joy."
"Are there no teardrops where you live?" I asked.
"I have traveled the world," he said.
"There is no dwelling where they never fall.
Trust, hope and love will dry tears."
I smiled and said, "I choose Joy."

Acrobat

Gray squirrel who eats my nuts and seeds
Enjoys his lunch and runs away
Never waves or says "hello"
Something strange took place today
Somersaults and wild gyrations
Executed with success
I didn't see a squirrelly girl he was trying to impress
It may have been because it's spring
Fermented nuts or some such thing

Critique

I loved your phrases, neatly turned
The meter with proper impetus
Now the moment of truth has come
Methinks thou was ambiguous

Example

I had a visitor today
A "he" or "she" I do not know
Tiny ant on my kitchen floor
I must have dropped a crumb or two
It tugged and pulled its heavy load
In a moment it disappeared
No exercise room when it came home

Globetrotter

It stood upon a table, not very tall
Round and round it turned
Yellow, pink, blue and green
Teacher said, "This is the world."
"How small," I thought.
"I'm standing somewhere on this globe."
Names she read danced in my head
Oceans, countries, people
Blue water everywhere
So many lands, lines between
Ridges beneath my fingers
Mountains tall
Islands scarcely seen, rising from the ocean floor

My world, so small
A little road that led to school
Store, where rainbows of candy beckoned me
Past the vineyard where grapes hung, purple, come September
Trees I climbed, fields I roamed

I gazed at people on pages in my book
Children with black hair, dark brown eyes
Eskimos in igloos, clothed in skins and furs
Indians, beating tom toms, dancing in a line
Australians, shearing sheep, chasing kangaroos
Pictures have no life
I must believe it is true

Horizons widen with the years
Came the day when high above the earth
I looked down at ships upon trackless sea
Icebergs, floating free

Mountains that once were ridges under childish hands
Rose to majestic heights
The wonder of it all has not grown old to me

Once more, I'm standing near the globe
My teacher in her pretty dress

Faint perfume I remember well
She never knew she planted in my heart the seeds of wanderlust

I was a dreamer as a child. For many years
I had no hope of traveling to Europe. I knew
I had family in Switzerland. A man I met opened a
door of opportunity. I met several family members.
In my dreams I live it again.
B.P.

Love Story

Love is not a perfect day
Sometimes there are clouds of gray
Love is looking in your face
Seeing sunshine through the rain

Love is not always orchids
Though orchids there may be
Love is a primrose, wet with dew
You pinned it in my hair for me

Love is not always smiles
Though smiles may appear
Sometime love is a tender touch
That fills my eyes with tears

Love is not always glitter
Though glitter there may be
Love is the sunset that we share
As we walk along the sea

Love is not a song
Though I hear music in the air
A melody of angels
I sense your presence everywhere

Love is not a limousine
With shiny paint and leather fine
Love is just to walk with you
And know that you are mine

Love is not gold or jewels rare,
Though diamonds there may be

I'd give them all away
If you'd chase rainbows with me

Love's not a feast in a castle
Dining with kings and queens
Love is a chocolate, only one
A bite for you, a bite for me

Sometimes love is just seeing you
I do not ask for more
I don't have words to tell you
I've never gone this way before

Love is not always youth
Time will flee away
My darling, I'll hold you in my heart
As dear to me as you are this day

Are you planning your wedding day?
If you have a friend with a gifted speaking voice,
you are welcome to include "Love Story"
in your wedding ceremony.
B.P.

Wisdom

Wisdom is better than strength.
Strength shall fail, hands become feeble.
The wise are never alone.
They feast upon their storehouse of remembrance.

Wisdom is better than weapons of war.
When swords are broken, guns silent,
That which was built is gone,
Wisdom shall build again, for it survives.

Wisdom is better than riches.
Silver and gold may lose their value.
The wise know that wealth alone
Never satisfies a selfish heart.

Wisdom loves truth.
Deceit has no strong foundation.
Wisdom given as an inheritance,
Remains to enrich the earth.

Psalm 90:12 – Teach us to number our days aright, that we may gain a heart of wisdom.

Proverbs 24:3 – By wisdom a house is built and through understanding it is established.

Proverbs 10:23 – A fool finds pleasure in evil conduct, but a man of understanding delights in wisdom.

Requiem for Pretense

The brightness of her smile embraced the room.
Sparkling words like Roman candles,
It was the summer of her life.
The façade hid dark recesses of her soul.
Tears at midnight, dried at dawn
Living with yesterday, today had no meaning.
Why should there be a tomorrow?

She chose her final farewell,
sleeping as the hourglass of time ran out,
leaving her still and cold.
Who would have guessed?

No tomorrow.

Requiem

The sun was shining when he left
Hiding tears as he walked away
I couldn't let him see
He had taken part of me

Acceptance

They came, both young and old
Forgotten ones
People of the street
Some with hope nearly gone
Now and then, a spark of life
Deep inside, hidden now from sight,
There lives a child with wonder in his eyes,
Who reaches out with trusting hand
Broken by the storms of life
Sometimes I see a glimpse of hope.

My child, it matters not to me that hands are dirty, clothes are worn
One day He walked the dusty roads
No place to lay His head

As they came; the poor, the blind and lame
He did not say, "Come back when you are clean."
The cleansing that He gives is of the heart.
When the heart is clean, I'll see the child again.

Memories of time spent with "street people."
B.P.

The Inheritance

He followed his father in the field.
The little feet, two steps for every one
"How do you catch a rainbow, Dad?
"There's a pot of gold at the end."
"I never found it, son.
To see the rainbow is enough for me."
As years passed, he watched his father plant the corn.
The hay was in the barn.
"Dad, why don't you sell the farm?
You've labored long and hard."
"Son, my father cleared this land.
He felled the trees.
The stones made yonder fence.
If you should be so blest to have a little boy someday,
Perhaps in that field he will find the pot of gold."

Have you misplaced something carelessly
because you didn't realize its value?
Some people have sold possessions
for a few dollars, later to discover
they were irreplaceable.
B.P.

Farewell

The tree nearly barren, I sadly whisper goodbye.
The final leaves waving, as if to say,
"See you in springtime in a new gown."

Words Unspoken

Lifetime of words: so many spoken
Could it be those left unsaid may be the most precious of all?

In Retrospect
Pearl Harbor

Polynesian trade winds
gently touch
small marble stones
row upon row

Unknown – December 7, 1941

Punchbowl – crater of the dead

My tears fall
for
unknown mothers

Secret Places

"I'm building a house," you said.
"It will be finished soon, please come."
The dream fulfilled, I stood in wonder.
Birds filled the trees with song.
The path, with flowers like jewels
Windows, sparkling like sunbeams
You have seen this in your dreams for a lifetime!
I saw your smiling face as you opened the door.
Loving care was written in each room.
"Thank you for sharing with me," I said.
Looking into your eyes, my heart said, "I do not know you.
"Please invite me into your home, the one you live in."
Hinges no longer open that door; the lock is filled with rust.
One day, long ago, I thought I saw you.

It was only a moment.
I may have dreamed it.
The windows; covered with dust
I cannot look inside.
I'm sure there is treasure no one has seen.

As I slowly walked away
I heard you softly say,
"Come back another day."

Diagnosis

Pale and worn
She lay at rest
Fingers on pulse
Another test

The best of care
Newest drugs
No one ordered
Loving hugs

Pain she felt
Long concealed
Lonely heart
Unrevealed

Repose

"Take no thought for your care," He said.
"A sparrow is not forgotten.
I will feed and clothe you.
Walk in the field where lilies grow.
They toil not nor spin
Their beauty surpasses king's robes.
Rest in peace, my child."
Luke 12:27

Moving

We were heavy-hearted as we waved goodbye
The house where we had lived so many years
Fields where flowers bloomed and berries grew
The tree house that we built where enemies dare not climb
Friends whose secrets we had shared

Unfamiliar roads we had never seen
Life takes so many turns –
Curves have hidden it from view

My childhood left behind these may years
I wanted, once again, to see that special place
I looked for landmarks that once I knew so well

Other hands have changed the things I loved
I looked, in vain, for friends
They, too, had traveled other roads

I may never come again, but
I can climb the tree house in my dreams
and fight the tigers
in the grass

Flowers

I saw him, ragged and worn
His eyes tired, lines upon his face
He didn't appear to be someone who would buy flowers
Were they for a mother, old and forgotten?
For someone living with pain?
His beloved, in an everyday world?
The message, "I love you."
Memory for a lifetime
Remember when you gave me flowers?

The Song

I heard it in a nearby tree
A song so sweet I stopped in wonder
Surely, a bird of rare beauty, I thought
I searched in vain for one whose song had changed my day
A flash of gray, almost unnoticed
As if to say
"If the song is sweet, it matters not who sings it."

A Candle in the Dark

You, against all odds, come into being?
Among millions, you are unique.

The mystery of life eludes us,
thus we substitute that which has no meaning

A choice; to love or hate
To blaspheme or worship
The thirst for knowledge sometimes leads
down roads of confusion

To beloved Daniel was revealed at the
End time, "many shall run to and fro and
knowledge shall be increased."

To what end?
For millenniums
Winter and spring
Summer and autumn
Sun and moon in their appointed pathways

Happenstance?

Diamonds formed in darkness
Their brilliance revealed the light

In the miasma of dark despair, hope's candle burns brightly,
Illuminating shadows on the journey to eternity.
In the face of death, platitudes disappear.
Some choices are ours to make, others in the Creator's hands.
He is the Keeper of Promises.

Daniel 12:4

Friend

You had faith in what I could become
Courage when I was weak
You listened when others turned away
The power of love transcended fear
Because you came, a golden thread was woven into my life
My wilderness became a garden of blossoms
Dear friend, rare and precious

Family Album

Undisturbed upon the shelf
Generations of faces
Some I have never seen
Born in distant lands that had no power to hold them
Crossing oceans to weave a dream
Fears and hopes in the crucible of life
Faces forever young
No record of how it was and how it will never be again
A locked door with no key

Reality

I cannot match the face to the child inside.
Changes came slowly, youth reflected no longer.
Dreams vanished in a cloud on a lonely road.
Times past, I polished them often.
They gleam no more, viewed through the eyes of reason.

Expectation

I would approach you without prejudice
A risk-taker
Having neither sword nor shield
I do not plant flowers and expect weeds

Resurrection

The storm passed by
Rain had washed teardrops of mourning from my eyes
At my feet, blossoms pushed through last year's leaves
Resurrection

Adversity

The pearl glowed softly; flawless and elegant
The result of suffering and frustration
One grain of sand invades the creature in the shell
It strives to force the alien out
Resistant and abrasive, the invader remains
Resigned, the creature coats the sand with luster
Resistance becomes acceptance
How many tragic lives radiate beauty?
We will never know
They have covered their grief
Ashes, watered with tears, have grown bright blossoms.

*Many years ago I read about a man who
had entered bankruptcy five times before
he became successful. As I consider those
who bravely conquered almost impossible obstacles
as pioneers, I am amazed how many people
have lost the ability to endure hardships.
I cannot truthfully say I enjoyed some of my early life,
but it prepared me for situations I would later encounter.*

B.P.

Spendthrift

I was given golden coins the day I came.
The bag was full, one for every day of life.
I could spend them as I chose.
My mother's hands exchanged the first for a rocking chair and
pillows soft.
She spent it for tender smiles and loving arms.
Came the day when I chose for myself.
My hands were filled with gaudy trinkets, forgotten long ago.
The coins dropped slowly, time became the misty past.
Some went for school days, happy times with friends.
I had so many left, I spent them carelessly.
Coins for perfume and saucy curls
Dreamy days and fairy tales
Moonlit nights and starry skies
At last, coins for a tiny house
Cookies
Curtains in the breeze
Once again, a baby's smile
A bag of coins into her hands
Not mine to spend
So few of mine remain
Oh, that I could say
"Spend them wisely, child."
It seems I hear a whisper from long ago,
"You shall not pass this way again."
In one grand gesture
I spent them all for love.

Tomorrow

Every day she swept the porch
She waved as I drove by
An ordinary lady
No one to catch your eye

She didn't wear the latest style
Her house was plain and small
I knew her name was Mary
Nothing else that I recall

"Mary, would you feed my dog?
I can't get home tonight."
"Of course, I'll do that," Mary said
As I drove out of sight

The neighbor just across the street
With children, two and four
"Mary, would you watch the girls
While I go to the store?"

The summer sun was blazing hot
Mary came with lemonade
A neighbor, pushing his lawnmower
"Jim, drink this; Come, sit in the shade."

Spring, summer, autumn, winter
Another year is past
"I must send flowers to Mary."
Tomorrow; time disappears so fast

The little house is silent
A note upon the door
Mary left this world last night
We won't see her anymore

Final goodbye in the quiet room
Our tearstained eyes on her gentle face
Flowers we arranged in her careworn hands
Yesterdays we can't replace

Justice

Mama didn't wear a robe
She had no gavel in her hand
She could deal with problems
As wise a judge as any man

We tried to keep the trouble quiet
Far from Mama's eyes
"Kids, get in the house!"
There wasn't any compromise

"You sit on that chair!
You sit over there!"
We couldn't touch each other
We pretended that we didn't care

We weren't allowed to say a word
Whining and crying were in vain
Two hours sitting on a chair
Make enemies good friends again

Ancient History

My brother was a rascal
Two years younger than myself
Mama sent us to the store
To carry groceries home
At age thirteen he didn't care
His clothes were dirty, shoes a disgrace
No polish; I cleaned them with cod liver oil
He smelled like a fish market walking
Many years later I visited him
For me, he charcoal-broiled a steak
Did that mean he had forgiven me?

Sometimes

If I had wings the tallest tree would be my resting place
I'd build my nest high, where breezes would rock me to sleep
I could view the river on its merry way to join the bay
The fisherman, at early dawn, drifting on the quiet lake
Blue herons wading in the morning mist

Horses, in the pasture, running wild and free
A farmer, bronze from hours in the sun, plowing long furrows
Crimson rays of setting sun reflected from cottage
windows down the lane

Sometimes when the day is dark and I am all alone
I close my eyes and fly until I reach the highest branch
Then, swooping low become a butterfly bright and beautiful
Sometimes

Alone

I wander along a hill and in a glen
A remnant of last year's leaves
They whisper softly as I pass by
An echo of autumn's glory

Melancholy thoughts

A glance beyond, moss awaiting warm
Spring showers; a velvet carpet

I live again fairy tales, so loved,
when leprechauns lived in such a glen as this

Prince searching for a princess fair,
charging through a forest glade

I cannot hear the fairy wings, the chargers have all disappeared

My thoughts are mine alone

How can I explain?

No one to see or hear

Sheepherder

Flat prairie land, shimmering heat waves
Distant hills on the horizon
Far away on the prairie, small covered wagon,
gleaming white in the sun

Keeper of sheep
Faithful dog, never wandering far
What kind of man is this?
Silence; except for bleating of sheep
Gentle binding of wounds and bruises
Soft breeze, sometimes harsh winds
His companions
Sun and rain, thunder and lightning

Washing dusty clothes, splashing in the stream
Mealtime; boiling coffee, opening cans

Grazing scarce, time to move on
Shearing; harvest of summer

Dew, sparkling diamonds at sunrise
Streaks of crimson at sunset
Prairie bathed in moon glow
Constellations like old friends

Long summer days fade into autumn
Across the lonely prairie, shelter for winter

Small western town; lonely room
Does he dream of the sun on his back, the soft lowing
of sheep at sundown?

Winter Delight

Snowflakes, whirling and dancing with whimsical wind
Resting lightly on branches and rooftops
Through the dark, silent night, snow's mantle covers earth's blight
The world appears newly created
Morning sun changes snow crystals into diamonds

Children's faces at window panes
Pure delight

Doors fly open
Warm coats, hats and mittens
Happy voices calling friends

Snow angels on pristine snow

On to the lake!

Impatiently clearing ice
Lacing skates with flying fingers
Bright faces reflecting sunbeams
Waltzing and swaying

The sun climbs toward noon

Smoke ascending from chimneys
Hot chocolate and peanut butter sandwiches

Nail Soup

When I was only a little child
Many years ago
I heard a story about a tramp
His name, I do not know

A tramp is simply a homeless man
Who wanders here and there
He doesn't go to work each day
He eats and sleeps most anywhere

One day he walked along a road
Nothing else to do
The sun was hot, his feet were tired
He was hungry, too

He saw a pretty cottage
"A place to rest," said he
"Perhaps they have a bowl of soup
they would share with me."

He knocked upon a bright, green door
Footsteps, then a woman's face
"Have you some food for a hungry man?"
"Nothing," she said; "Try another place."

"If you have nothing to eat," said the tramp
"I'll make you a wonderful treat.
Give me water and wood for a fire
I'll cook something for us to eat."

The woman stared in disbelief
"I have water, wood and a pot," she said

The old tramp quickly built a fire
As she watched and shook her head

From village houses round about
Mothers and fathers, children and dogs
Came running to watch the excitement
Water boiling on crackling logs

From his pocket he took an old rusty nail
Dropped it into the pot and stirred
No one had ever seen such a sight
They all stood spellbound, not saying a word

"What are you doing?" a little boy asked.
"Making nail soup, it's wonderfully good.
It would be much better with an onion or two
Meat, to taste as it should."

"I have onions," a woman replied.
An old farmer offered to bring some meat
"A bit of salt to make it taste better."
Said the tramp; "This soup can't be beat."

Salt, meat and onions went in with the nail
The old man stirred as he smiled with delight
"With carrots it would be fit for a king
A few carrots would make it just right."

Eager hands held bounty to add to the feast
Fire danced brightly, faces aglow
Children playing, neighbors laughing
Celebration of joy that happy hearts know

Soup like this, in wonder they marveled.
The tramp called, "Bring your bowl and spoon!"
Amazing what a nail will make
He filled their bowls as he whistled a tune
The tramp pulled the nail from the empty pot
Into his pocket he dropped his treasure
Evening shadows fell as he waved goodbye
No doubt, somewhere, his nail soup brings pleasure

Mystery

The washer washes, the dryer dries
The freezer freezes fruit for pies
The mixer mixes chocolate cakes
The toaster toasts, the oven bakes

Grandma pumped water, scrubbed the clothes
Half a day's work before the sun rose
Fed the chickens, planted some seeds
Picked the beans, pulled some weeds

When a neighbor dropped in from down the road
She visited while some stitches she sewed
It's a mystery to me as I run pell-mell
How Grandma had time to "set a spell"

Tale of Woe

Don't marry a man who goes fishing
Especially if you have little money
Rods, reels and a leaky old boat
Nothing left for flowers and candy

No motor, only a pair of oars
Guess who rows the boat?
"We are in too close, row over there."
No brakes, we've drifted close to shore

Three inches of water, my feet are wet
Bail out water, sink or swim
One tiny fish, too small to keep
Sunburn, windburn, mosquito bites

A bowl of soup and I'm going to bed

Sea of Life

Waves, rolling endlessly
Against the horizon, nearly a mirage, a ship slowly appears
Nothing to announce where it has traveled or its home port
At peril of sea and storm the Captain steers toward His destination
Thus am I upon the Sea of Life
Although I have a chart and compass,
Tumultuous waves have forced me off course
My Captain, beside me, aware of danger threatening;
His hand upon the wheel sets a course of safety
My destination; a country I have never seen
I have read of its beauty, unseen by mortal eyes

Darkness surrounds me
Rain descending in torrents
Clouds cover my vessel
Can it be, harbor lights in the midst of the storm?

Do you know someone who never has a problem?
Some storms of life are expected; others,
suddenly with no warning. I read again the account of
Jesus and his disciples, crossing a lake, in the midst
of a storm. Jesus sleeping, his disciples fearful of drowning.
Awakened, He calmed the storm. He has not changed.
-Luke 8:22-25
B.P.

Unknown

Who carried wood to the high rocky ledge to build
a lighthouse, decades ago?
Does anyone remember their names?
Rugged men who challenged death far below
What of the lighthouse keeper?
The same narrow stairway, day after day
Polish the lens and glass
Light the flame
Crimson sunset or raging sea spray

No one needs beams from a lighthouse when the
sun is shining bright.
Ships sail past with scarcely a thought of the man who keeps watch
through the night.
He never knew the lives he saved.
Somewhere, a weathered old captain and mate
remember fierce storms.
Nearing the rocks, recall the bright gleam, nearly too late

Not always to heroes our debts we owe.
Sometimes to strangers we'll never know

Garage Sale Junkie

If you should come to visit me
Don't get too close or stay too long
I have the strangest malady
It may be contagious, there's something wrong

It forces me to wake at dawn
Jump in my clothes and run
No time to eat my breakfast
It's still too early for the sun

My pockets jingle with quarters and dimes
I've circled addresses with a big red mark
Here's the street and there's the house
Oh dear, there's scarcely room to park

I've developed the garage sale lope
That moves me right along
If I don't hurry fast enough
The treasures will be gone

A pretty dish, a tablecloth
A pair of shoes in a box
A thingamajig and a whatchamacallit
And a little chest that locks

When I came home with my treasures
I couldn't get in the door
Next week I'll have a garage sale
Before I buy anymore

Transition

I lived in a shack
Long time ago
Dug in the garden
With shovel and hoe
Cardboard on walls
Cracks around windows
A junky, old ~~chair~~ car
Hand-me-down clothes
I sang as I worked
Smiled at the sky
Didn't have money
Didn't ask why
Now I need nothing
The road has been long
Surrounded with beauty
I still sing my song

No Clones, Please

In all the world you are unique.
There's no one quite like me.
We're on this earth together.
If we should disagree
Be thankful we're not all alike.
How boring life would be!

Carousel

Only a nickel
For a ride
With longing eyes
Softly she cried

Horses prancing
Glittering gold
Pockets empty
Seven years old

Fifty years later
Gray hair flying
Music playing
Grandma went riding

*Is riding a carousel only a memory from
the distant past? Perhaps you know
a little one that rarely has a special day.
View the world through eyes of wonder.
Decades past they will live again that wondrous day.*

B.P.

Equality

"The profit of the earth is for all.
The King himself is served by the field.
He that loveth silver shall not be satisfied by silver,
Nor he that loveth abundance with increase.
This is also vanity.

Ecclesiastes 5:9, 10

Wise the man who lives with contentment.
The poorest and richest are warmed by the same sun.
The finest grain may be eaten in a hovel or palace.
Earthen bowls or fine china
Fruit delights paupers and kings
All eyes may feast upon beauty.
Dwellers in mansions live with loneliness as do seekers of wealth.
Some have starved with pockets of gold.
Greed begets greed.
The sun rises and sets.
Rain falls and winds blow.
Some forces are beyond men's control.

God is on the Throne

When the moon gives no light
When stars and planets fall
The earth melts with fervent heat
Faults in the earth shift and destruction covers the land

God is on the throne

When tidal waves sweep the shores
Ships tossed like matchsticks
Locusts devour grain in the fields
Blighted fruit falls from trees

God is on the throne

When men curse and blaspheme God
Hearts are filled with greed
Men refuse to kneel before the One who died for them
The righteous are called foolish

God is on the throne

When Satan is cast into the bottomless pit
Heaven is filled with music and singing
All sorrow is forgotten,
Tears are wiped away

God is on the throne

Summer Storm

mumbling
and
grumbling,

flashing
and
crashing

howling
and
growling

and

only a
few
drops of rain

Chameleon

Sun or shadows
Lethargic and warm
Hidden 'neath leaves
Dr. Jekyll and Mr. Hyde
Lunch anytime
No cooking
No dishes to wash

Changes

The crooked, old tree
Was cut today
Among the flowers
It quietly lay
The birds appeared
As if to say
"Why did you take
our friend away?"
The scenery's changed
To avoid mishap
The squirrels must print
A new road map

Spider

Busy spinner, master designer
Swinging in space on bridges of air
Waiting for dinner; guests invited
The menu?
"Please, take that chair."

The Dreamer

When the perfect moment?

Baby hands and smiles, the touch of angels,
Nestled safe and warm, protected with love

Tender days of childhood
Blowing silk from dandelions to make a wish
Chasing a shadow you will never catch

Sixteen
Dazzled by dreams of a handsome prince
He rode past to another kingdom.

The radiant bride at twenty
Forever happy days before cold winds of reality erased the glow of
tenderness

Can this be the little girl, standing at the altar where once I stood?
Years past but a moment in time

The mirror reflects joy and sorrow
Time; a giver of gifts who snatches them away

When the perfect moment?

I remain a dreamer.

Someday

Unforgettable words
Received with joy
Others that linger with devastation
Heartbreak that rises above joy as waves in a swift current

Someday

Tender words of love between Jesus and me
Words I have never heard
"Come, my child, I have been waiting for you."

I shall remember no more the unforgettable

A love to die for
Forever

An amazing statement from a small,
adopted child to another child held
by her mother: "My mother chose me."
B.P.

Altered Dreams

If I could buy a dream, what would it be?
I need some time to contemplate.
If you had asked me years ago, my answer would have taken hours.
Poverty gives birth to wondrous dreams.
The Midas touch:
Flirtation with gold
Morpheus left no precious gifts.
The sun rose, the gate to Paradise was closed.
The princess was no more.
The mirror reflected only rags.
No prince, no coach
I was a builder of castles that crumbled.

If I could buy a dream today, what would it be?
The essence of life
A heart engraved, forever unaltered
Love and serenity

A Child's Treasure

Myriads of daisies like drifting snow
Petals falling as breezes blow
Each flower; in the center, a coin of gold
I gathered as much as my pocket would hold

Hidden Treasure

Far beneath the earth, crystal streams flow although
I have never seen them.
Their abundance waters my garden.

Walking in a field and forest I may have crossed veins of coal.

Pools of oil, undisturbed for centuries; covered by rolling prairie sod

Tons of ore from rugged mountains yield only a tiny vial of gold.

Diamonds from hidden places, sought for perfection
Too valuable to wear, they are locked in vaults.

Shop windows gleam with opals, rubies and sapphires

Men have traded lives, love and honor for what
they could not possess.

How sad!

They must leave it all behind.

I have no treasures locked away.
The One who placed them in the earth
reserved the finest for that heavenly
city I shall someday call "home."

Horizons

Some would choose prairies
Windswept, limitless horizons
Blaze of copper at high noon
Baked parched earth
Oasis of heat waves
Trees, struggling to survive
Battered dwarfs with ungainly arms
Stretching to catch a stray raindrop
Endless day fades into twilight
A crescent of platinum
The moon sails high
Crickets' evensong, a prairie concert
As for me,
I love the view from the top of a hill.

Darkness of Night.

Sunrise.
I have never understood how a tiny bird
senses the light when I see only darkness.
On a mountain, in a forest or meadow
"Good Morning" in birdsong, a delight.
B.P.

Investment

Gnarled old fingers, a tiny coin
She gave it without measure.
A widow's mite in the hand of God
Surpasses rich men's treasure.

Creation

The night is dark.
No moon, no stars
Firefly
Light in the darkness
No battery, no fuel
Who said, "There is no God"?

I saw a firefly last night.
BP

II Samuel 11 & 12

Solomon
What compelled you to write words of wisdom rather
than wield a sword or spear?
Thoughts which contemplated life
Seeker of answers
Aren't we all?

Your heritage
David, your father; from a shepherd to a king
A young man who killed a giant but betrayed a man of valor.

Why seduce the beautiful woman Bathsheba, wife of your defender,
Uriah?
Forbidden in the sight of God
Loyalty rewarded with death.
No defense against a king

What future for the child soon to arrive?

Nathan, God's messenger, chosen to confront
King David as a murderer
Facing the man who had life and death in his hands
The prophet's message, "The child shall surely die."

Satan does not reveal the carnage of sin; king's robes or beggar's rags.

David, prostrate before his God, fasting
Victories forgotten in Death's presence
Seventh day – the child, silently departing.

Accepting God's will, David's comfort
"I shall go to him; he shall not return to me."

David and Bathsheba's son, Solomon
Blessing from tragedy
His words of wisdom remain with us.

The dust returns to the ground it came from
and the spirit returns to the God who gave it.
Ecclesiastes 12:7

Beginning Again

My friend,
I call you friend though time has passed since we
shared hopes and dreams.
The friendship that was ours was not the ordinary kind.
It did not bind us with a heavy chain.
Rather, like a strand of gold, delicate but strong
We felt secure, bound by love's strong cord.
One day, in heat of anger, words you spoke
Like an arrow, pierced the golden strand.
It fell in pieces at our feet.
You turned away without farewell.

Your letter came today.
The words were swift and sharp.
Tearstains on the page were from your broken heart.
I cried aloud; the wounds were deep.
I can't erase the words we said that day.
Once spoken they live on in memory.

Will you meet me on the street, "Beginning Again"?
The empty place that once you filled is empty still.

Sentimental Journey

Bits and pieces of life
Fingers that stitched quilts no longer thread needles
In memory, I see Grandma in her chair, rocking babies, piecing quilts
"Don't throw it away, I'll put it in a quilt," she said, as she placed it in
the chest her father made as a wedding gift.
"I remember when Grandpa wore that shirt."
Grandma saved the shirt tail when the collar frayed
"Aren't those pieces from Aunt Amy's apron she wore
at summer canning time"?
Grandma sewed aprons to wear over Sunday go-to-meeting clothes.
"Mary Ann wore that dress when she was two."
Pieces of blue from Johnnie's shirt; he now has sons of his own.
Elizabeth's cheeks were as rosy as the flowers in that piece.
"Elizabeth, do you remember that pinafore"?
Daisies
"You were six and I was eight when we wore our daisy dresses."
Pieces of tablecloth recall happy faces around the table, fried chicken
waiting as we bowed our heads.
Scraps of pink gingham from kitchen curtains, long forgotten
"Edith, Grandma saved pieces from the dress you tore on the fence."
As children, we did not cherish our heritage.

The chair is empty.
Thousands of stitches, sewn with loving hands,
invite us to a sentimental journey.

Exodus

I have caught a glimpse of heaven.
Through poverty and broken dreams, disappointment
and storms of life
Its beauty has not grown dim.

Hope surrounds me.
Love dries my tears.

Spring
Summer
Autumn
Winter

Gone are the days when I wished time away.

A lifetime long past
Time and maturity bid me walk an unfamiliar road.

Sunrise and sunset blend into mist
Each moment a treasure

The Unknown

A blend of tears and raindrops
Taste of life like bitter herbs
Longing for a place unknown

Life's hopes shattered like dust on a country road.
Shadows at eventide
Façade of a smile that becomes a tear.
Where does one search for hope?

The majesty of our King rules the universe.
Wind and waves respond to His command.
Sun and moon cross a trackless sky.

Forgive me, Lord.
I sought escape, not understanding.
There is peace in your presence,
A secret place from the trouble that surrounds me.

The path you chose for me, I do not understand.
This I know;
You are a keeper of promises.

*Rich or poor, humanity cannot
escape problems. What comfort
to know the Lord understands.*

B.P.

Coming Home

By faith, Abraham, when he was called to go out into a place which he should after receive for an inheritance, obeyed; and he went out, not knowing whither he went.
Hebrews 11:8

Houses I have lived in and left behind
Not homes, merely houses
Something always missing

Time to move on
No weeping, for I shall someday find that perfect place.

Centuries removed, Abraham searched for a city he never found;
Not content with the ordinary.

A wealthy man
Endlessly pulling tent stakes, moving a family and possessions
Something always missing

Longing without understanding

Until I behold the celestial city, I, too, search for that which I have
never seen.

"Abraham, someday we shall be home at last."

Farm? No, Thanks.
Bertha Phebus

"How would you like to care for a farm for six weeks"?

On a November day in 1947 my husband Dale came home from work with this unusual question. He then gave me a hard sell on the advantages. We had sold our large, old home and purchased a house trailer. Before Dale had been discharged from the United States Army in 1946, he was stationed in Washington State, and we had decided to move there from Michigan in the spring. Our daughter was four years of age.

Dale said Louie, a man he met at work, needed someone to care for his farm while his family went to Florida for a six-week vacation. Of course they wanted to leave when the weather was coldest. Louie said we could live in their comfortable, ranch-style house and have all the milk and eggs we wanted. They would also pay us a small amount of money. Louie said there wasn't much work involved. He said Dale could take care of it in a couple of hours, morning and night. Six cows were to be fed and milked; there were two beautiful riding horses, and their daughter had a pony and colt.

It goes without saying that where there are animals, the end result is manure, which must be shoveled and spread on fields. There were several large hogs. Dale went to the bakery for returned and damaged bread to mix with mash and water to make slop. I had to water and feed fifty chickens, collect and clean their eggs, and place them in cartons.

Dale worked from eight until four at a manufacturing company. Louie said that after chores, he could do as he liked. Louie's wife Garnet introduced us to Bill, an old man from Ireland who lived with them – a patient from the state hospital. The state paid the Saboes to keep him. Although harmless, Bill had a mental problem and could not care for himself.

I was young – twenty-three – and had always worked hard. I knew that I could easily care for a large house, feed and water chickens and gather eggs. To live in a beautiful house with a fireplace in cold weather was much more appealing than living in a small trailer. The day of their departure came. At the last minute Garnet informed me that Bill enjoyed eating and sitting in an old rocking chair. He did not want to do anything, but because he needed exercise, I was to send him out twice a day to check on the animals.

She left the name and telephone number of a veterinarian if there should be a problem. We moved in and waved goodbye. Dale did the chores before he went to work and when he arrived home. I enjoyed the modern comfortable house while our daughter had fun playing with new toys.

When Garnet told me Bill liked to eat, I had no idea how much. The pancakes disappeared like snow on a July day, along with bacon, eggs, juice, toast, and coffee. He moved from the table to the rocking chair with no evidence he intended to check on the animals. I had been taught to be kind to older people. At first I gently suggested he look around the barns. He continued to rock. It always took an hour to get him motivated.

A few days later Dale complained that he had pain in his back. By the end of the day he said he couldn't walk. To say I was dismayed was an understatement. I didn't know one thing about cows and milking machines. Dale limped out to the barn and instructed me. When cows lie down, they don't check for a clean place. The cows' udders had to be washed thoroughly with soap and water and rinsed. Unfortunately, the udders are under the cow. I don't know if my hands were cold or the cows knew I was inexperienced, but they kicked and switched their tails constantly. Attaching a milking machine was not fun and games. I never really became friends with those cows.

The hay was stored high in the hay loft. That meant climbing an old ladder and throwing down bales of hay, morning and night. Shoveling manure is not one of my favorite hobbies. I had never thought much about what happened to what was left when the cows finished with it. The body heat from the cows helped to warm the barn. I couldn't say much for the perfume, a la manure. I had been warned not to startle the horses because they were high spirited and would kick me. I made plenty of noise when I opened the barn door. I was scared to death – more oats, hay, water, and manure.

Dale did manage to go after bread for the pigs. When it was time to mix the slop, I unwrapped the bread and added it to the mash and water in a big metal barrel, using a large shovel. The hogs wandered in a big field. The moment they heard the shovel hit the barrel, they came running. I tried to pour pails of slop over the fence, but they squealed and jumped against the fence, splashing slop over the ground, on my mittens, coat and boots. From then on, I was quiet as a mouse until I had put the feed over the fence.

I can't truthfully say I enjoyed taking care of the chickens. When night came, the chicken house became very cold and water froze in the pans. Chickens eat, then drink, repeating the process over and over. The water becomes thick with mash, making the pans difficult to clean when they freeze. I carried hot water from the house to melt the ice and filled pans with the oyster shells necessary for strong egg shells. Beautiful eggs in cartons don't come that way from the chickens. They don't wipe their feet when they enter the nest to lay eggs. Water removes the protection that keeps them fresh. I used fine sandpaper to clean them. When I tried to reach the eggs under the hens, they resented my intrusion. I had many wounds for which I received no commendation.

Rats like the chicken house because food was always left in the feeders. I bought something my father had used – electric paste – and cut small pieces of bread. The paste came from the tube smoking and had a horrible smell, but it made the rats crave water. They left the building. The paste was supposed to dry their bodies and kill them. They did disappear. I don't know if they dried or drowned in the river. I didn't go to look.

Ten beautiful, white ducks lived near the river. They had a little house with a fence so they wouldn't swim away. Much to my sorrow, at feeding time nothing was left except feathers, orange bills and feet. I never knew what ate them. It was a dismal sight.

All chores had to be repeated morning and night. I scarcely had time to do laundry, shop, and cook. The weather had been cold but not unbearable. One day the radio announced an arctic freeze was on the way. The next morning the thermometer read twenty-three degrees below zero. I went to the barn to feed animals and milk cows. The water pipes were frozen. Have you any idea how much water one cow drinks? Multiply that by six. When I thought about watering cows, horses, pigs, and chickens, I could scarcely face it. I had to carry pails and pails of water about one hundred feet to the barn. I came to the conclusion I must be from hardy peasant stock.

One day I went to the barn to clean manure only to find there was no manure behind one of the cows. I knew something was wrong and called the veterinarian. When he came, he said it was a rare problem. I knew it would be if it happened to me. One intestine had telescoped into another. Dr. Smith said he couldn't do anything. The cow was diseased, but she would die soon; however, the meat was safe to use. He gave me the name of a company who would butcher the cow immediately. I felt disturbed about having someone else's cow butchered, but there was a bright side – one less cow to feed, water, and milk.

With much persuasion, Bill checked the barn twice a day. I was in the basement doing laundry when the back door flew open. Bill shouted, "Missus, the hogs are out!" The farm was located near a busy highway, and I was petrified by visions of hogs causing accidents. I said, "Bill, the hogs can't be out. How could that happen?"

I didn't wait for an answer. I grabbed my hat, coat, boots, and mittens and ran. The snow was deep. Bill had left the big gate open. I was chasing hogs, scolding Bill, yelling and running as fast as possible. When the hogs came almost to the gate, they turned and ran the other way. A neighbor finally helped me get them back in the field.

I knew the sows were going to farrow soon, but I didn't know when. Perhaps running caused one of the sows to have her litter of tiny pigs. All but one was dead. I picked him up and ran for the house. Wrapping him in a towel, I put him in a warm oven. When I took him out, he was dead. He was so tiny and perfect; I was sad to think I couldn't save at least one.

Miraculously, Dale's back was much better by the time the Saboes returned. Sometimes I hear people relive fond memories of life on a farm. If someone gave me a farm today, there would be a "For Sale" sign on it tomorrow.

CPSIA information can be obtained at www.ICGtesting.com
Printed in the USA
BVOW05s1852271014

372551BV00001B/5/P